PAKISTAN UNDER SIEGE

Pakistan Under Siege

Extremism, Society, and the State

MADIHA AFZAL

BROOKINGS INSTITUTION PRESS
Washington, D.C.

Copyright © 2018
THE BROOKINGS INSTITUTION
1775 Massachusetts Avenue, N.W., Washington, D.C. 20036
www.brookings.edu

The Brookings Institution is a private nonprofit organization devoted to research, education, and publication on important issues of domestic and foreign policy. Its principal purpose is to bring the highest quality independent research and analysis to bear on current and emerging policy problems. Interpretations or conclusions in Brookings publications should be understood to be solely those of the authors.

Library of Congress Cataloging-in-Publication data are available.
ISBN 978-0-8157-2945-7 (pbk.: alk. paper)
ISBN 978-0-8157-2946-4 (ebook)

9 8 7 6 5 4 3 2 1

Typeset in Galliard

Composition by Westchester Publishing Services

To my parents
Farkhanda and Wasim

And my husband and son
Salik and Amahl

Contents

Preface

Over the last ten years, tens of thousands of Pakistani civilians and security forces—25,051 by one count—have been killed in terrorist attacks conducted by the Pakistan Taliban and other militant groups.[1] Is terrorism in Pakistan a manifestation of a society moving toward radicalism or one victimized by terrorist groups created by geopolitics? Are ordinary Pakistanis extremists?

In the West, Pakistan is characterized as a villainous, failing state that created a terrorism monster and does not do enough to fight it; it is, thus, blamed for the hazards its citizens face as well as the danger it poses to the rest of the world.[2] Its citizens are thought to be irrational fundamentalists. This book takes issue with that characterization. Pakistan has its demons and more, no doubt, but it has come to be defined exclusively in terms of its present struggle with terror, by the jihadist training camps in Pakistan, and the links of some Pakistanis to attacks in the West. Its story is far more complex.

In this book, I lay out the imperatives facing the Pakistani state, its strategic (mis)calculations, the attitudes of Pakistani society, and the country's turn toward extremism. I show how the Pakistani state has helped foster militancy in the country and how the exclusionary nature of Pakistan's Islamization—undertaken by the state more for strategic than ideological reasons, as part of its nationalist project—has mainstreamed extremist narratives. The Pakistani state has done this through manipulating the country's laws and education system. The state could not have imagined the enormous ramifications of these choices on Pakistan's society and on its security.

Pakistani society is multi-dimensional, but the world is most likely to see images of anti-American mobs or crowds who show up at rallies held by Islamist fundamentalists. On the other end of the spectrum is a liberal intelligentsia whose members, while small in number, have a significant voice in Pakistan, although one not often heeded in policy. And a large group of its citizens holds the middle ground.

What do average Pakistanis think of terrorists, of jihad, of militant groups? Are their views "radical"? In this book, I describe Pakistanis' views as understood from the results of surveys and interviews—including their views of terrorist groups and their understanding of their country's present struggle with terror, their views of religious minorities and non-Muslims, their perceptions of places beyond their country, and their understanding of their place in this world.

What explains how Pakistanis think? How has the Pakistani state—its politics, laws, and institutions—affected the trajectory of violent extremism in Pakistan and shaped its citizens' attitudes toward terrorism? Pakistan's politics—embodied in the interrelationship of its military, its democratic government, and its Islamist parties—defines the relative strength of these three power players; I identify the role each has played in Pakistan's slide toward extremism through each player's actions, narratives, and relationship with militant groups. I trace the evolution of Pakistan's laws and show a direct relationship between the regression of these laws and worsening citizen attitudes.

The Pakistani state has used its education system as a vital pawn in shaping its citizens' thinking. I identify the role that education—education in terms of years in school, of curricula in public and private schools, and of the much-maligned madrassa system, which is often blamed for fostering extremism in Pakistan—plays in defining attitudes on extremism. I do this through quantitative analysis of survey data, interviews with students in schools and colleges, and an in-depth study of textbooks and teaching.

Much of the current work on extremism in Pakistan tends to look at it from a detached position, from a top-down security perspective, limited to the actions of the state with little focus on how those actions affect the ordinary Pakistani. The historical underpinnings of the state's actions are too often ignored. We are left with a one-dimensional picture of a complex, richly textured country of 200 million people. In this book, using rigorous analysis, interviews, and a historical narrative, I fill out the picture of Pakistan's relationship with extremism. The methodological approach is novel. In the end, I hope to convince the reader that there is hope yet for this beleaguered nation.

Acknowledgments

This book is the culmination of several years of my research and writing on extremism, education, and politics in Pakistan. I would like to thank the people who helped me along the way here, as well as organizations—with my apologies in advance if I inadvertently miss some names.

The U.S. Institute of Peace (USIP) provided the initial research grant for my school fieldwork (in early 2013). Officials at the Punjab textbook board and at the curriculum wing in Lahore and in Islamabad helped me understand the curriculum landscape in Pakistan in a way that no official documents could. The Punjab education department facilitated visits to government high schools. Administrative officials at public, private, and nonprofit schools graciously allowed me and my team of two research assistants to spend days at their schools; teachers kindly let us sit in on their classes and generously gave their time for interviews. Mehwish Rani and Mohammad Ali were my wonderful, intrepid research assistants during the fieldwork. Above all, I want to thank the high school and university students who engaged in focus group discussions with us—I am immeasurably grateful for their openness with their views, for their willingness to give so much of their time to us, and for their generosity of spirit.

Over the years, I have presented various aspects of this work at universities and research institutions and have benefited greatly from the comments and questions of those in the audience, including presentations at multiple seminars at the public policy school at the University of Maryland (UMD) and a particularly helpful workshop at UMD's Department of Government and Politics in November 2016. Other events at the following institutions have been invaluable: Wilson Center, Center for Global Development, USIP, Brookings, University of California–San Diego, College of William and Mary, and the Center for Economic Research in Pakistan.

I have also written about some of this work in newspapers and online publications—especially the *Express Tribune*; Brookings blogs; *Foreign Policy*; *Newsweek*; *Cairo Review*; the *Washington Post* Monkey Cage blog—and have published two longer, related pieces as well: my USIP special report on education and attitudes in Pakistan; and a chapter in the Routledge *Handbook of Contemporary Pakistan* on curricula in elite and public schools. The publication of these articles, both short and long, helped clarify my thinking, and I profited from the feedback of readers.

I have also benefited from discussions with many colleagues at various institutions—especially Faisal Bari, Nancy Gallagher, Michael O'Hanlon, Bob Nelson, Anand Patwardhan, and Moeed Yusuf. Thanks also to Allen Schick, Carol Graham, Mac Destler, and Dave Crocker for their support.

My utmost thanks go to Bill Finan for his unwavering support of this book from the very beginning, for his patience, and for his wise counsel. Thanks also to Janet Walker and the entire team at

Brookings Press, and to Angela Piliouras at Westchester Publishing Services.

None of this would have been possible without the endless support and encouragement of my family—my parents, Farkhanda and Hassan Wasim Afzal; my son, Amahl; and my husband, Salik. This book is dedicated to them.

ONE

A Country of Radicals? Not Quite

Are ordinary Pakistanis radicalized? According to the most recent Pew polls, Pakistanis overwhelmingly oppose what some in the West call "radical Islamic terror"—that is, violence against civilians to "defend Islam from its enemies." Defending Islam and fighting for it: this is how terror groups such as al Qaeda and the Taliban justify their violence against civilians. It is part of their version of jihad.

In 2013, 89 percent of Pakistani respondents said such violence was never justified.[1] But in 2004, nine years earlier, only 41 percent of Pew respondents opposed such violence. More than a third— 35 percent—said it was justified (see figure 1-1). The trend over the years suggests it is Pakistan's own experience with large-scale terrorist violence—an abstract phenomenon before 2004 that became more widespread and multiplied in scale after 2006—that has driven Pakistanis' clear opposition to violence against civilians, even when in the name of Islam.

1

FIGURE 1-1. **Violence against Civilians Justified to Defend Islam?**

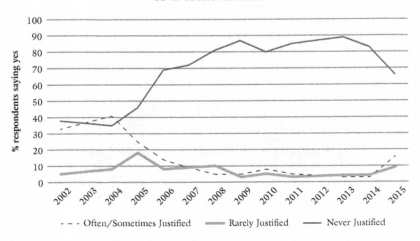

Source: Author's graph, using Pew Research Center's Global Attitudes survey data for Pakistan for the years 2002–15 (excluding 2003 and 2012; www.pewglobal.org/datasets/).

Interview Question: Some people think that suicide bombing and other forms of violence against civilian targets are justified in order to defend Islam from its enemies. Other people believe that, no matter what the reason, this kind of violence is never justified. Do you personally feel that this kind of violence is often justified to defend Islam, sometimes justified, rarely justified, or never justified?

Note: Only a small number of people refused to respond to this question or said they didn't know their answer (this was a problem for other questions), making this a particularly good question to study.

Does the average Pakistani sympathize with terrorist groups? Do his or her views vary according to the terrorist group—say, groups that attack Pakistani civilians versus ones that attack Pakistan's "enemy," India? What about those groups that attack the West and Western targets?

We will see that the majority of Pakistanis do not express sympathy with extremist groups—no matter who the group targets. But common narratives on terrorist groups—some riddled with conspiracy theories—paint a less positive picture. This chapter sets forth the survey evidence and common narratives on how Pakistanis think about terrorist violence and militant groups, including al Qaeda, the Taliban, and Lashkar-e-Taiba. Related to these views are citizens' perceptions of India, of the United States, and of Pakistan's place in the world.

A WORD ON THE DATA

Before we go forward, let me say a few words on the survey data. For Pakistanis' views on terrorist groups, I primarily analyze the data from the Pew Global Attitudes surveys conducted annually in Pakistan (and other countries) since 2002. Pew conducted face-to-face interviews with adults eighteen years and older in Pakistan. In most years, approximately 1,200 individuals were surveyed; in 2002, 2007, and 2010, about 2,000 people were surveyed.[2] Until 2006, Pew conducted interviews in Urdu; after 2007, in Urdu and regional languages. The polls are nationally representative of 80 percent to 90 percent of the population; Pew excluded regions that were insecure. Their sampling was disproportionately urban, but I weight the results to account for Pakistan's true urban/rural composition.[3,4]

Polls typically suffer from a number of common problems, and the Pew surveys are no exception. Respondents may not be truthful and, instead, may choose the socially desirable response (social scientists refer to this as social desirability bias); or they could refuse to answer specific, sensitive questions—with the result that we may not know what many respondents think, and our results may be biased because those who refuse to respond may systematically conceal specific views (this is termed nonresponse bias). An advantage of the Pew polls is that they offer an unparalleled timeline on Pakistanis' views, allowing us to trace attitudes from shortly after 9/11 to today.

I complement the Pew data with data from the Program on International Policy Attitudes (PIPA) poll, conducted in May 2009.[5] This survey used careful question wording and enumerator training to successfully deal with sensitivity concerns, yielding low nonresponse rates to a set of sensitive questions. All interviewing was conducted in Urdu, with 1,000 face-to-face interviews across a hundred locations in rural and urban Pakistan.[6]

I also use data from the Pew Forum on Religion and Public Life, a multi-country survey on religion and society conducted in Pakistan in November 2011. This survey was also conducted face-to-face, with about 1,500 adults, and was nationally representative of 82 percent of the adult population.

A (VERY) BRIEF PRIMER ON PAKISTAN-RELEVANT TERRORIST GROUPS

Here, I briefly introduce the four militant groups we consider in this chapter: the Pakistan Taliban, the Afghan Taliban (AT), Lashkar-e-Taiba (LeT), and al Qaeda (AQ).

The Pakistan Taliban, also known as the Tehrik-e-Taliban Pakistan (TTP), was founded in December 2007 by Baitullah Mehsud, a semi-literate village imam, as an umbrella organization of smaller outfits in Pakistan's tribal areas; its principal target is the Pakistani state. The group has attacked politicians, military and intelligence targets, and police academies. It has also attacked civilians—women and children—in mosques, schools, hotels, parks, and churches. It has posed the main threat to Pakistan's security for the last ten years, and continues to do so today, though it has been significantly weakened by the army's operations against it since 2014.

The Pakistan Taliban claims to fight the Pakistani state's alliance with the United States in the war in Afghanistan and the Pakistani military's post-9/11 crackdown on militant outfits in the country's tribal areas. It aims to remove Pakistan's democratically elected government and to impose Sharia. The group is closely allied to but distinct from the Afghan Taliban. It pledged allegiance to Mullah Omar—the head of the Afghan Taliban whose death was disclosed in 2015, two years after he allegedly died at a Pakistani hospital, according to Afghan officials—as its own supreme commander but has its own set of managing leaders.

Some members of the Pakistan Taliban became radicalized from their involvement in the jihad against the Soviets in Afghanistan in the 1980s. In 1989, Sufi Muhammad, who had fought in that jihad, formed the Tehrik-e-Nifaz-Shariat-Mohammadi (TNSM) to impose Sharia in Dir. The TNSM was one of the precursors of the Tehrik-e-Taliban Pakistan. His son-in-law, Fazal Hayat, known publicly Mullah Fazlullah or just Fazlullah, is the current leader of the Pakistan Taliban. He is a former chairlift operator with no formal religious training. In chapter 2, I discuss the rise of the Pakistan Taliban.

The Afghan Taliban is an Islamist fundamentalist group that came into power in Afghanistan in 1996 after years of fighting between various groups of mujahideen (Soviet war–era fighters) over control of post-Soviet Afghanistan. As groups of mujahideen fought for control of Afghanistan in the 1990s, Benazir Bhutto's government made a decision to back the Afghan Taliban in its bid for power; she later admitted she and her government had made a mistake. Mullah Omar headed the Taliban until the announcement of his death. The Afghan Taliban ruled Afghanistan with regressive, draconian interpretations of Sharia. It required women to be covered head to toe in a burqa; women and men were treated at separate hospitals; men were required to wear beards; music and television were banned. Anyone in violation of the Taliban's rules was punished severely, often in public.

Post-9/11, the Afghan Taliban was ousted from Afghanistan by the United States' invasion of that country; members of the group sought sanctuary across the border in Pakistan and many, including the leadership, are thought to be in Quetta—although Pakistan officially denies this. Over the last fifteen years, the Afghan Taliban has attacked American forces, and Afghan government and civilian targets, from its reported base in Pakistan. It is fighting against the United States and the U.S.-backed Afghan government in Afghanistan.

Pakistan treats the two Talibans very differently. It has engaged in a military operation (Zarb-e-Azb) against the Pakistan Taliban since June 2014 even as it continues to give sanctuary to the Afghan Taliban. The Pakistani state justifies this sanctuary, though not openly, as giving Pakistan leverage and "strategic depth" to insure against fears of Indian involvement in Afghanistan.

Lashkar-e-Taiba is one of the main anti-India militant groups based in Pakistan, fighting to free Kashmir from Indian control. Jaish-e-Mohammad (JeM) is the other. These groups do not attack the Pakistani state or Pakistani targets; they target Indian forces in Kashmir, and government and civilian targets in India. These groups, the Kashmiri jihadists, began functioning at a heightened capacity in the 1990s; they drew from the ranks of the mujahideen trained for the Soviet jihad once that war ended. Scholars and analysts argue that Pakistan's spy agency, the Inter-Services Intelligence, harbors ties with and supports Lashkar-e-Taiba and Jaish-e-Mohammad and that it directed the mujahideen toward the Kashmir cause. Though the Pakistani army denies this, it is well known in Pakistan that despite these groups being proscribed, their leaders are largely allowed by the state to conduct their activities and live freely. The head of LeT is Hafiz Saeed, an erstwhile engineering university professor. The charitable arm of Lashkar-e-Taiba, Jamaat-ud-Dawa (JuD), is widely visible (see box 1-1 for details).

Al Qaeda is well known globally. It was the terrorist group led by Osama bin Laden, responsible for 9/11 and a host of mass-casualty terror attacks at high-profile Western targets. It is now led by Aymen al-Zawahiri. Its jihad is global, against the United States and the West. Osama bin Laden was killed in a U.S. Navy SEAL operation in Abbottabad, Pakistan, in May 2011. He had been living there for several years but how he wound up there and who knew he was there is unclear. Given that Abbottabad houses Pakistan's military academy, it is likely that at least someone in Pakistan's intelligence agencies knew.

BOX 1-1   Jamaat-ud-Dawa's Charity

Hafiz Saeed is quoted: "Islam propounds both dawa [prosely-tizing] and jihad. Both are equally important and inseparable. Since our life revolves around Islam, therefore both dawa and jihad are essential; we cannot prefer one over the other."[a]

Jamaat-ud-Dawa runs schools and ambulances and organizes emergency relief. By 2009 it claimed to run the second largest ambulance fleet in Pakistan. At that time it also ran 173 al-Dawa educational institutions with about 20,000 students.[b] After the devastating October 2005 earthquake that hit Kashmir and Pakistan's northern areas, JuD was at the forefront in providing relief to those affected. It provided effective medical care from well-stocked field hospitals it had established after the earthquake. The *Washington Post* reported from Muzaffarabad that the JuD field hospital there had "X-ray equipment, [a] dental department, makeshift operating theater, and even a tent for visiting journalists."[c] After the massive 2010 floods, *The Telegraph* reported that JuD provided "food, medicine and wads of rupee notes to hundreds of thousands of people affected."[d]

a. Stephen Tankel, "Lashkar-e-Taiba: Past Operations and Future Prospects," New America Foundation: National Security Studies Program Policy Paper, April 2011, p.3.
b. Ibid., p.12.
c. John Lancaster and Kamran Khan, "Extremists Fill Aid Chasm After Quake," *Washington Post*, October 16, 2005.
d. Rob Crilly, "Pakistan Flood Aid from Islamic Extremists," *The Telegraph*, August 21, 2010.

While the four militant groups discussed—the TTP, the AT, LeT, and AQ—are distinct, and function separately in Pakistan, their boundaries blur. Foot soldiers cross over and ideologies overlap. All invoke Islam; all want to enforce Sharia. What varies is their geographical focus: whether it is national or regional in scope. Their targets of violence are correspondingly different. For al Qaeda, it is the West; for the Afghan Taliban, U.S. forces in Afghanistan and the Afghan government; for the Pakistan Taliban, the Pakistani state; and for Lashkar-e-Taiba, the target is India. The Pakistani state effectively treats these groups differently from each other, only recognizing the Pakistan Taliban as a threat, and even that only in more recent years. But how do Pakistani people see these militant groups? Do they recognize the common militant threat? Do they sympathize with the common ideology? Or do they discriminate according to who the group targets?

PAKISTANIS' VIEWS OF TERRORIST GROUPS: WHAT THE POLLS SAY

Polls show that Pakistanis are, on balance, unfavorable toward all terror groups, including those that do not attack Pakistani civilians, such as the Afghan Taliban, Lashkar-e-Taiba, and al Qaeda. That does not mean that no Pakistanis hold favorable views of these groups, but rather that more of them are unfavorable toward these groups than not. A sizable section of respondents refuse to answer questions about these groups, but whether the nonresponses conceal views that are favorable or unfavorable is not clear. Nonresponses may vary by location or be dependent on specific factors like the respondents' perceptions of the pollster asking the question. Respondents could also truly be indifferent or not have enough information to answer the question.

Views vary somewhat across groups, as can be seen in table 1-1. Pakistanis are more positive toward the LeT than other terror groups (14 percent say they have favorable views of LeT) but the number is still small. Favorability toward al Qaeda is the lowest across terror groups (7 percent) and is 9 percent for both the TTP and Afghan Taliban. Thirty-six percent of Pakistani respondents say they have unfavorable views toward Lashkar-e-Taiba. Unfavorability is

Table 1-1. *Pakistanis' Views of Terrorist Groups*

| | Percent | | | |
Response	Tehrik-e-Taliban Pakistan*	Lashkar-e-Taiba*	Afghan Taliban*	Al Qaeda**
Very favorable	3	3	3	0
Somewhat favorable	6	11	6	7
Somewhat unfavorable	17	13	16	15
Very unfavorable	43	23	37	32
Don't know/refused to respond	30	49	38	45

Source: Pew Research Center Global Attitudes Pakistan survey dataset, spring 2015 (www.pewglobal.org/datasets/2015/).
* Interview Question: Please tell me if you have a very favorable, somewhat favorable, somewhat unfavorable, or very unfavorable opinion of: a) TTP, b) LeT, c) AT. (Pew has fielded this question since 2010.)
** Interview Question: And thinking about some political leaders and organizations in our country, please tell me if you have a very favorable, somewhat favorable, somewhat unfavorable, or very unfavorable opinion of al Qaeda. (Pew has fielded this question since 2008.)

highest for the TTP (60 percent), and lower, at 53 percent, for the Afghan Taliban and 47 percent for al Qaeda. Nonresponse rates are high for LeT, AT, and AQ—between 38 percent and 49 percent—and lower for the TTP (at 30 percent).

Across terror groups, Pakistanis express the most negative views of the Pakistan Taliban, the group that directly targets them and the Pakistani state, and also have the highest response rates to questions about the TTP. If fear of terrorist groups alone motivated nonresponse, it would be highest for the TTP, given its imprint in Pakistan. That we see such high unfavorability and low nonresponse despite the TTP's terror suggests that the high nonresponse rates for LeT, AT, and AQ may, in fact, reflect ambivalence.

The views of the TTP discussed here were recorded in 2015, a few months after the December 2014 attack on the Army Public School in Peshawar, which was thought to have significantly hardened Pakistanis' views against the militant group. Before the attack, in 2013, unfavorable views toward the TTP were already very high, at 56 percent; they went up slightly in 2015 to 60 percent. The bigger change seems to be lower favorability post-attack (from 16 percent in 2013 to 9 percent in 2015), and somewhat higher nonresponse. It is interesting that views changed not only for the group that perpetrated the attack—the TTP—but also for the LeT, whose favorability declined from 24 percent in 2013 to 14 percent in 2015, and AQ and the AT whose favorability also declined after the Peshawar attack (from 13 percent and 12 percent in 2013 to 7 percent and 9 percent in 2015 for AQ and the AT respectively). Similarly, unfavorability went up slightly for these groups, and nonresponse rose somewhat, as well. To sum up, Pakistanis were already very negative toward the TTP before the Peshawar attack, and they turned further against the TTP as well as other terror groups after the attack.

Looking back, Pew respondents' views on the TTP did not change much between 2010 and 2013. A Pew question that asks respondents about their views of the Taliban—without the Pakistan qualifier but prefaced with a statement that the question is about "organizations" that function within Pakistan—has the advantage of being asked since 2008. A look at that data shows that Pakistanis' views on the Taliban changed significantly between 2008 and 2009; nonresponse and favorability declined and unfavorability rose dramatically—both as Pakistanis learned more about the group and as they became targets of its terror.[7]

This change in views between 2008 and 2009 also holds for al Qaeda. Pakistanis became less favorable, less nonresponsive, and more unfavorable toward al Qaeda between 2008 and 2009. Combined, this evidence suggests that as Pakistanis were increasingly targeted by terror they became more unfavorable toward all terror groups, not only the group that struck them directly. For al Qaeda, nonresponse has risen and unfavorability has fallen after 2012, as the terrorist group has become less of a global threat after Osama bin Laden's death.

We have another snapshot of views of al Qaeda with the PIPA data in 2009, and with better response rates. PIPA ascribed its lower nonresponse to asking respondents about bin Laden's organization (*bin Laden ki tanzeem*) rather than al Qaeda (the word *Qaeda* may be confusing to Pakistanis, since it means literally *book* or *guidebook*; and while some respondents may not have known the organization al Qaeda by name, they had heard of bin Laden). This data suggest more positive views toward al Qaeda in 2009 than the Pew surveys—with 27 percent of PIPA respondents reporting positive feelings, 16 percent mixed, 45 percent negative. Twelve percent did not respond. For comparison, Pew in 2009 reported 9 percent favorability, 61 percent unfavorability, and 30 percent nonresponse. We cannot come to a definitive conclusion with one comparison point, but this suggests that, for al Qaeda, nonresponse may have disguised positive or favorable views.

Data from surveys other than Pew and PIPA confirm these findings. In a 2009 survey of 6,000 Pakistanis, a group of academics (Graeme Blair, C. Christine Fair, Neil Malhotra, and Jacob N. Shapiro; henceforth referred to as the BFMS survey team) used endorsement experiments to mitigate nonresponse and to derive truthful views of militant groups.[8] They asked their respondents about the Afghan Taliban, al Qaeda, and Kashmiri jihadist groups (but not the Pakistani Taliban). Their results show that Pakistanis are on average negative toward these groups—corroborating my findings.

What about ISIS, a growing player in Pakistan? In 2016 and 2017, it was responsible for multiple large-scale attacks across Pakistan, although in some cases it appears to have "outsourced" these to other militant groups—including Lashkar-e-Jhangvi, a Sunni sectarian group. Pew asked a question on ISIS in 2015, but 62 percent of Pakistani respondents did not answer it. Nine percent of respondents were favorable toward the group, and 28 percent reported unfavorable opinions. That nonresponse rate likely reflects lack of knowledge or ambivalence about the group, thus we cannot yet reach a conclusion about Pakistanis' views on ISIS.

It is clear that Pakistanis disapprove of extremist violence, but denouncing terrorists' ideology is a different matter. Both the polling data and citizens' narratives make this apparent.

NARRATIVES ON TERRORIST GROUPS, AND AMERICA, INDIA, AND ISLAM

Pakistanis' views on al Qaeda are closely tied to their views on the United States; their views on Lashkar-e-Taiba to their views on India. In what follows, I describe their narratives on these two countries, relying on further survey data and interviews, and relate these to their views on the terror group that attacks either country. Next, I lay out deeper narratives on the Taliban based on open-ended interviews and show how these narratives, in turn, relate to and are driven by Pakistanis' views on India, on America, and on Islam, jihad, and Sharia.

Al Qaeda and America

For al Qaeda, two things are simultaneously true: a clear majority of Pakistanis do not support its attacks on the United States, and a majority of Pakistani respondents sympathize with al Qaeda's attitudes toward the United States (see table 1-2). Sixty-two percent of PIPA respondents said they opposed al Qaeda's attacks on Americans, but 34 percent of respondents said that, while they opposed such attacks, they nevertheless shared many of al Qaeda's attitudes toward America—that is, more than half of the 62 percent of respondents who oppose attacks said they still shared al Qaeda's attitudes toward the United States. Twenty-five percent of respondents said they supported attacks on Americans (clearly disturbing) *and* shared al Qaeda's attitudes toward the United States—

Table 1-2. *Al Qaeda Attacks and Values*

How do you feel about al Qaeda?	Percent
I support al Qaeda's attacks on Americans and share its attitudes toward the U.S.	25.44
I oppose al Qaeda's attacks on Americans but share many of its attitudes toward the U.S.	33.58
I oppose al Qaeda's attacks on Americans and do not share its attitudes toward the U.S.	28.06
Don't know/no response	12.92

Source: Program on International Policy Attitudes Pakistan 2009 survey dataset.

adding up to a total of 59 percent of PIPA respondents who said they shared al Qaeda's attitudes toward America. Twenty-eight percent of respondents said they opposed al Qaeda's attacks *and* did not share its attitudes toward the United States.

These attitudes are undoubtedly linked to Pakistanis' unfavorable views of the United States. I discuss these next.

The United States

Figure 1-2 shows Pakistanis' views of the United States since 2002. Views are clearly unfavorable (unfavorability never falls below 50 percent), but these numbers have varied over the years. The low for unfavorability was 56 percent in 2006—attitudes toward the United States were boosted by American aid in the wake of the massive 2005 earthquake in Pakistan and Kashmir[9]—and the high was 80 percent in 2012—the year after three major events (the Raymond Davis incident, the Osama bin Laden raid in May, and the November NATO attack that killed twenty-four Pakistani soldiers) severely undermined the United States' standing in Pakistan. Davis was a CIA contractor in Lahore who, while driving on a crowded street in that city, shot and killed two men on a motorcycle in January 2011. A U.S. consulate car dispatched to help him then killed another man while driving on the wrong side of the road. Pakistan arrested and charged Davis, but after the American and Pakistani

FIGURE 1-2. **Pakistanis' Views of the United States**

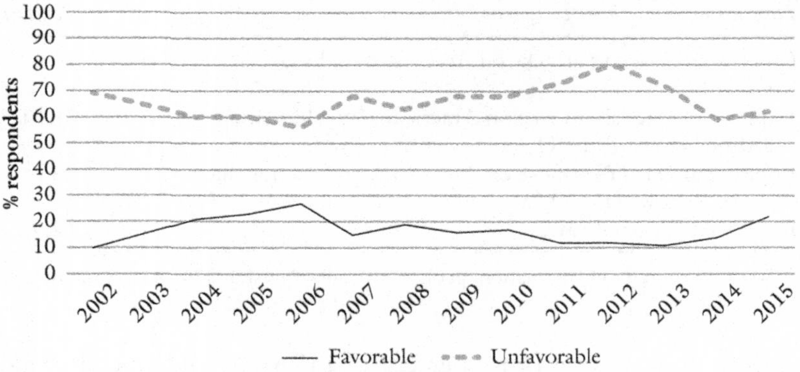

Source: Author's graph, using Pew Research Center's Global Attitudes survey data for Pakistan for the years 2002–15, excluding 2003 (www.pewglobal.org/datasets/).

governments reached a deal to pay blood money to the victims' families, he was cleared of all charges and flown out of Pakistan. American authorities are said to have pressured Pakistan into that agreement with the possibility of Congress holding up its civilian aid.

Polling data and interviews yield a picture of Pakistani anti-Americanism that, with help from a classification system developed by prominent political scientists Peter Katzenstein and Robert Keohane, we can delineate into four different categories—radical, socio-religious, sovereign-nationalist, and liberal (although these categories are not exclusive or nonoverlapping).[10]

Underlying a socio-religious anti-Americanism in Pakistan are notions of a conflict between Islam and the West and that of "Islam in danger" from the West. The narrative posits the American superpower pitted against the Muslim world, with Pakistan's identification and sympathy firmly ingrained on the side of other Muslim countries (it is the old "us versus them" argument). Polls reveal that Pakistanis think it is a "U.S. goal" to "weaken and divide the Islamic world" (78 percent of PIPA 2009 respondents) and to "impose American culture on Muslim society" (79 percent of PIPA respondents). High school students I interviewed in

Punjab confirmed these views. One said: "They can't see Islam rising. . . . America doesn't want Muslims to survive in Pakistan, in fact not in the whole world." In the words of another: "America and other countries—their main aim is to divide and rule, to finish our unity."

Pakistan's strain of sovereign-nationalist anti-Americanism, on the other hand, focuses on American policies seen as harming Pakistan, as impinging on its sovereignty, and as unfair to it. Pakistanis consider the United States to be a bully who is unfair to their country. Ninety percent of PIPA respondents said that, in their view, the United States abuses its greater power to make the Pakistani government do what it wants (as opposed to treating Pakistan fairly). In the words of a student I interviewed, "We are America's slaves." My interviewees often called on the Raymond Davis case as an example of a strong-handed America impinging on the sovereignty of a weak Pakistan. In this context, they almost always contrasted the fate of Aafia Siddiqui with that of Davis. Siddiqui was an MIT-trained Pakistani neuroscientist who was suspected of having links to al Qaeda and to the 9/11 attackers. She "disappeared" for five years between 2003 and 2008. She was taken into custody in Afghanistan in 2008 and, shortly after that, attempted to kill American security officers guarding her; she was convicted by a New York court on charges of attempted murder in 2010 and is serving an eighty-six-year sentence in the United States. But she is a *cause celebre* in Pakistan: Pakistanis are skeptical of her links to terrorists, believe her to have been held in American custody and tortured in the years she was missing, between 2003 and 2008, and to have been driven insane by this torture. It is a case of two sides—American and Pakistani—seeing two completely different angles to the same story. Pakistanis of all types—including politicians—defend Siddiqui as the "daughter of the nation" and argue for her to be returned to Pakistan.

Pakistanis also keenly feel that the United States favors India over Pakistan when it comes to America's relationships in South

Asia (53 percent of Pakistani Pew respondents in 2015 believed American policies toward India and Pakistan favored India; only 13 percent said they favored Pakistan). They also feel that America sides with India in the India-Pakistan conflict and in the two countries' nuclear ambitions, although Pakistan is, in fact, the official U.S. "ally." A popular narrative invokes the economic sanctions imposed on Pakistan after it responded to India's nuclear tests with tests of its own in 1998; these sanctions were deemed deeply unfair to Pakistan. This kind of episode feeds Pakistan's mistrust of America and its sense of betrayal.

Pakistanis are also acutely sensitive to what they perceive as American operations that violate their sovereignty. In the Pew survey conducted immediately after the Navy SEAL raid that killed Osama bin Laden in May 2011, 63 percent disapproved of the raid. Pakistanis also have no tolerance for U.S. counterterrorism operations on their territory despite agreeing with those measures on principle. As an example, almost 90 percent of respondents to the PIPA poll thought al Qaeda training camps and Afghan Taliban bases should not be allowed to exist in Pakistan, yet 80 percent of respondents also said the United States would not be justified in bombing such camps or bases.

Drone strikes—deeply unpopular—also fit into this sovereign-nationalist narrative. Fifty-five percent of Pakistani Pew respondents in 2012 had heard (a lot or a little) about drone attacks. Of these, nearly all (97 percent) thought drones were "a bad or very bad thing," and that they killed too many innocent people (94 percent of respondents). Three-quarters of respondents said that drone strikes were not necessary to defend Pakistan from extremist groups. More Pakistanis think such strikes are being conducted without the approval of the Pakistani government than not. While nonresponse rates and (lack of) knowledge of drone strikes are a concern here, the polls reveal a population wary of violations of Pakistan's sovereignty and civilian casualties in drone strikes. Pakistanis look at drones as yet another example of what they see as a blatant American disregard for Pakistani lives.

Liberal Pakistani anti-Americanism focuses on America's perceived hypocrisy in saying one thing and doing another, and on failing to live up to its own liberal and progressive goals and ideals. Examples of American actions that generate such sentiments in Pakistan are the failure to close down Guantanamo Bay and propping up dictators in contexts where it suits its own interests to do so, including in Pakistan. Sixty-six percent of PIPA respondents said that the United States tries to promote international laws for other countries but is hypocritical because it often does not follow these rules itself. Liberal Pakistanis tend to disapprove of U.S. foreign policy, both as it concerns Pakistan and the wider Muslim world—overlapping with strains of the socio-religious and sovereign-nationalist arguments. That manifests in disapproval of U.S.-led efforts to fight terror; 62 percent of Pakistani Pew respondents in 2011, for example, said they opposed such efforts. Liberal Pakistanis are also deeply skeptical about U.S. drone strikes and their cost to innocent Pakistani citizens.

Al Qaeda's narratives against the United States follow from the socio-religious anti-American argument, though some may resonate with those with sovereign-nationalist and perhaps even liberal anti-American sentiments. Only a person ascribing to a radical anti-Americanism, however, would support al Qaeda's violent extremism toward the United States.

Overall, Pakistanis are negatively predisposed to the United States, and their attitudes toward the United States range from mistrust to bias. These attitudes have deep historical roots and continue to evolve with current events that get woven into the anti-American narrative in Pakistan. One important aspect of this narrative deals with the anti-Soviet Afghan jihad of the 1980s, which Pakistan and America (and Saudi Arabia) together supported. Pakistanis cite American withdrawal from the region, characterized as abandonment, in the 1990s (leaving Pakistan to deal with a swarm of Afghan refugees, among other problems, on its own), as a form of deep betrayal.

Yet all is not negative when it comes to Pakistanis' views toward America. Pakistanis crave American approval and respect; their views do change with events and aid; and they admire America's successes—economic, political, scientific, and technological. And while the main story on Pakistanis' attitudes is their rejection of violent extremism, sympathy for the underlying ideology of extremists targeting America remains a concern.

Lashkar-e-Taiba and India

Recall that 20 percent to 25 percent of Pakistanis say they have favorable views of the LeT, according to Pew—a higher proportion than for al Qaeda, the TTP, or the Afghan Taliban. Nonresponse rates are high, as well, but the main takeaway is still the dominance of negative views over positive views of the group. This is despite the fact that the group has made deep inroads into the provision of charity via Jamaat-ud-Dawa, that it functions openly in Pakistan (at least its charity and political fronts do), and that the Pakistani state does not officially acknowledge LeT's role in terror. Given this, nonresponses may actually conceal respondents' lack of understanding about the significance of the LeT as a terror group. Consider, for example, that an injured man whose two children died in the 2005 earthquake in Muzaffarabad, Kashmir, said, after receiving care from Jamaat-ud-Dawa (according to the *Washington Post*), that he "did not know whether the group was involved in violence, nor did he care." What mattered to him was that "every 10 minutes a doctor or medical attendant comes in to check on me. I have a very high opinion about this organization."[11]

Pakistanis believe that the Indian occupation of Kashmir is illegal, that on the eve of partition, the Hindu raja of Muslim Kashmir went against the wishes of his people to accede to India. Pakistanis believe that Muslim Kashmiris are harmed by Indian rule, and they support self-determination for Kashmir. Thus the cause of Lashkar-e-Taiba naturally resonates with them.

There is also some evidence that Pakistanis ascribe goals to the LeT that go beyond fighting for the Kashmir cause. The results of the 6,000-person BFMS survey mentioned earlier reveal that respondents, in large majorities, ascribed the following goals to Kashmiri militant groups: fighting for justice, for democracy, to protect Muslims (and ridding the ummah of those who have abandoned their religion, or apostates).[12] Smaller numbers—large minorities to small majorities—of respondents also ascribe these goals to AQ and the Afghan Taliban.

In the Pakistani narrative, a pro-Kashmir stance goes hand-in-hand with an anti-India posture. India is deeply unpopular in Pakistan. Seventy percent of respondents reported unfavorable views of India in the Pew 2015 survey. This is unsurprising given that the two countries were formed after the breakup of the British-ruled Indian subcontinent in 1947. Partition was traumatic, and India and Pakistan have fought three major wars since then—two over Kashmir and another in 1971 over the secession of Bangladesh from Pakistan—and relations have frequently plummeted to other near-wars. There are plenty of warmongers in both countries, and the dispute over Kashmir—unlikely to be resolved—continues to be the primary bone of contention.

Each country considers the other to be its greatest enemy and threat. Asked by Pew to assess threats posed by specific groups and countries to Pakistan in the spring of 2014, 75 percent of Pakistani respondents saw India as a serious threat, while 62 percent said the same for the Taliban and 42 percent said that for al Qaeda. Asked to choose between the three, 51 percent stated that India was the greatest threat to the country, relative to 25 percent who identified the Taliban and 2 percent who named al Qaeda. In 2015, after the Peshawar attack, the percentage that viewed the Taliban as a serious threat increased to 73 percent, but respondents still considered India a greater relative threat than the Taliban, albeit by a smaller gap than in 2014: 46 percent compared to 38 percent. For reference, Indian views are a mirror image: in a 2011 Pew poll, 65 percent of Indians had unfavorable views of Pakistan and 45 percent viewed Pakistan as the greatest threat to the country when asked to choose between it, Lashkar-e-Taiba, Naxalites (members of the Communist party of India's Maoist group engaged in an insurgency against the Indian state), and China; many Indians consider LeT to be an agent of Pakistan.

In Pakistan, there is a pervasive sense that India is out to get it. The anti-India narrative starts with anti-Hindu sentiment before partition (the very reason for which was the fear of domination by a Hindu majority), extends to perceived unfair division of assets immediately following partition, to India's role in Bangladesh's secession from Pakistan, and to its unyielding stance on Kashmir. Pakistanis consider India to be a bully and Pakistan a victim.

Despite the likely resonance of LeT's anti-India stance with Pakistanis and the fact that they see more to the group than its actions against India, their rejection of the militant role of LeT is clear from the survey data (though this is presumably why we see higher favorable numbers for LeT than for other militant groups).

It is also worth noting that Pakistanis' anti-India views are not immutable. There is movement in the numbers: unfavorability has ranged over the years between a low of 56 percent in 2013 to a high of 82 percent in 2011—ebbing and flowing with tensions on Kashmir and the intensity of the nationalist rhetoric on both sides. Pakistanis and Indians both want relations to improve between the two countries. Seventy percent of Pakistani respondents in 2015 favored talks between India and Pakistan.

Before moving on to Pakistanis' narratives on the Taliban, it is important to briefly discuss their views on Islam, jihad, and Sharia.

Jihad, Sharia, and Islam

Pakistanis are religious, and many seem to believe in a version of Islam that is exclusionary. Ninety-two percent of Pakistani Pew respondents thought Islam is the one true faith leading to eternal life in heaven, though it is worth noting that the corresponding numbers for Egypt, Iraq, and Morocco are even higher.[13] Eighty-five percent of Pakistani respondents said Muslims have a duty to try to convert others to Islam.

Pakistanis are favorable toward Sharia (Islamic) law. In the November 2011 Pew poll, 84 percent of respondents said they favored making Sharia the official law of the land in Pakistan. Only 41 percent believe the laws in the country currently closely follow Sharia, but 71 percent think the way most people live their lives in Pakistan reflects the Hadith and Sunnah (the Prophet's sayings and practice); that is, they believe people are religious but the laws are not completely Islamic. Pakistanis believe, in overwhelming majorities, that a system of Sharia provides services, justice, and personal security and eliminates corruption, according to findings from the BFMS survey.[14] Seventy-five percent of Pakistanis say Sharia allows women to work, and 83 percent say it allows girls to go to school, according to data from the PIPA 2009 poll. Thus they understand it to be a system that enforces good governance and fairness.

What do Pakistanis understand of jihad? A plurality thinks of jihad both as an internal (personal) struggle and as involving violent action. Forty-five percent of respondents in the BFMS 2009 survey said jihad is both a personal struggle for righteousness and a struggle to protect the Muslim ummah through war, and about 25 percent said it is each of those interpretations alone.[15] The view of jihad as an armed struggle plays an important role in the Pakistani psyche.

21

NARRATIVES ON TERROR AND THE
PAKISTAN TALIBAN

Pakistani narratives on the terror the country faces at home—mainly at the hands of the Pakistan Taliban (although sectarian groups play a significant role, and most recently, ISIS has become active)—are complicated. What Pakistanis see is not as simple as terrorists striking at the Pakistani state and killing innocent civilians while claiming to implement their distorted version of religion. This would be something straightforwardly condemnable.

Instead, their narrative is confused, and their finger of blame does not point at the Taliban alone. Sometimes they recognize that the Taliban is responsible, but they also absolve it of blame. At other times, they call into question the very existence of the Pakistan Taliban as an autonomous group. Here I lay out some narratives that hold across Pakistan, illustrated at points with quotes from interviews I conducted with a large set of high school students and teachers in Punjab (more on these interviews in chapter 4).

A popular Pakistani narrative draws a direct link between the post-2001 U.S. "war on terror" and terrorism in Pakistan. This argument is simple and one-sided; it says the Pakistan Taliban is conducting attacks in Pakistan in retaliation to the U.S. war in Afghanistan and in response to American actions such as drone strikes in the tribal areas, as well as the Pakistani military's attacks against the Taliban in these areas. The argument goes that the U.S. war is not Pakistan's war, and the Taliban is punishing the Pakistani government for its alliance with the United States. This argument is usually accompanied by language that indicates that the militants' actions are justified. As a Lahori shopkeeper interviewed by the author Anatol Lieven put it: "The Taliban are doing some bad things, but you have to remember they are only doing them in self defense, because the [Pakistani] army took American money to attack them."[16] This narrative aligns closely with the Pakistan Taliban's own narratives of defensive action, and it doesn't always draw a clear distinction between the Afghan Taliban and the Pakistan Taliban.

There is partial truth to this narrative, but a more complete explanation goes back to the Afghan jihad in the 1980s, and to the United States, Pakistani, and Saudi roles in that war, and to the mujahideen that returned to Pakistan from that war, as discussed later. Of course a complete version would not absolve the Taliban of blame nor justify sympathy for the Taliban's actions, yet the prevailing narrative seems to accord the Taliban that indulgence.

A second narrative on the Pakistan Taliban is a straight-up conspiracy theory—that the Taliban is funded (or trained or armed) by India and America, who want to destroy, destabilize, and embarrass Pakistan. A student I interviewed put this theory thus: "We say that bomb blasts are done by the Taliban . . . [but] the major cause is the Americans and the Indians . . . the American agencies and the Indian agencies." A corollary of this narrative holds that the Taliban cannot be [real] Muslims because "Muslims can never kill Muslims. International powers are involved," in the words of a high school teacher I interviewed. The argument draws on reports of "foreign" militants caught in the tribal areas— they are Uzbeks or Chechens; the rumors say that they are not circumcised, so they can't be Muslim. There is sometimes an elaborate reference to an article or a video that shows this conspiracy theory in action. "Let me tell you, there was a place they showed in America, where there were religious Islamic men (maulvis), with long beards, who were being taught the Quran, but they were all kafirs [nonbelievers]—they were being sent in the midst of Muslims to derail/sidetrack Muslims," according to a student I interviewed.

Even this conspiracy theory has roots in history, specfically the training of the Afghan mujahideen in the 1980s, leading to arguments that "America created the Taliban" and al Qaeda. A teacher I interviewed voiced this view: "These groups are formed and raised by the U.S. from their early age. . . . Like in Afghanistan they were told that they have to get freedom from Russia. Bin Laden till yesterday was America's friend."

A third narrative on terror, less common, says that the Taliban engages in terrorism in the name of Islam to establish "an Islamic system" in Pakistan. A high school teacher told me: "They want Islam too. It is the duty of Muslims to spread God's words. They are just fulfilling their duties. Now you can call them either terrorists or jihadis." Given Pakistanis' religiosity and support for Sharia, as well as their views of jihad as an armed struggle, it is not surprising that this narrative resonates with them.

These narratives mix together in people's views, similar to the terrorists' own pronouncements—in the words of a man interviewed by Anatol Lieven in the Mohmand agency, who put his views in the most succinct terms: "The Taliban just want to fight the American occupiers of Afghanistan and bring Islamic law, and everyone agrees with that."[17]

A high school teacher told me the following when I asked him about the causes of terrorism in Pakistan: "Write down CIA, MOSSAD, RAW. I will not say Taliban because the day we stop drone attacks they will stop terrorism because they are believers of God and Prophet Muhammad. The Taliban is being funded by India and Israel and we are being supported by America and we are just fighting with each other. Why is that this war is not ending? Because both parties (Taliban and we) are getting support from outside. It's our own fault."

The first two narratives are clearly connected with anti-India and anti-America worldviews, and a sense of Pakistani victimhood—as a victim of circumstances, and of India and America—is evident. The conspiracy theory narrative—that America is out to get Pakistan—can be linked to a socio-religious anti-Americanism ("They can't see Islam rising"). The defensive narrative on the Taliban's actions is connected with the sovereign-nationalist form of anti-Americanism ("When somebody kills one's family, like America does in FATA/Waziristan, then he/she has to take revenge").

Thus any Pakistani sympathy for the Taliban is either defensive or ideological. It is not, however, based on views of superior governance or any positive illusions about Taliban rule, at least according to polling evidence from the PIPA 2009 survey. That survey was conducted in May 2009 following the government's deal in March with the TTP in the Swat valley. In return for the militants laying down arms, the government had agreed to impose Sharia law there. The deal did not last long.

Seventy percent of PIPA's respondents said their sympathies were more with the government than with the Taliban; they had a fairly realistic view of the latter. Respondents had little faith in the Taliban's potential provision of public services or governance. They expressed more confidence in the government than in the TTP for providing effective and timely justice in the courts, at preventing corruption in government, and at helping the poor. (This is despite respondents not having much absolute confidence in the government. In the concurrent spring 2009 Pew survey, 67 percent of respondents thought the government was doing a bad job dealing with the economy, and 53 percent thought the government was a bad influence on the way things were going in the country.)

Soon after the Swat deal, a video emerged showing the Taliban flogging a teenage girl in the Swat valley; it was widely circulated and evoked enormous backlash by ordinary Pakistanis against the militants. The PIPA poll showed that respondents understood the Taliban's regressive treatment of women and children: around 80 percent of PIPA respondents said the TTP did not allow women to work and girls to go to school in the areas where they had control; 69 percent said they thought the Taliban did not allow children to get vaccinated in these areas.

Thus, Pakistanis' views on Taliban governance are clear-eyed, and were so even in its early days. And many do denounce the Taliban. One of the students I interviewed said: "The Taliban are ruining the reputation and the name of Islam." But such denunciations of the Taliban can coexist with conspiracy theories or other narratives that promote misguided justifications for the militants' actions.

Pakistanis' views of terrorist groups are not as extreme as you may expect, but while Pakistanis are negative on militant groups and their violence writ large, their wider narratives surrounding these groups are far from simple. They clearly recognize extremism is a problem—82 percent of respondents in 2015 said they were concerned about "Islamic extremism" in Pakistan—yet their narratives on extremism are muddied by a sense of national victimhood, by a blindness toward Pakistan's own faults, by anti-American and anti-Indian sentiment and a deep-rooted sense of a struggle between Islam and the West. Adding to the confusion are strong ideological and religious convictions and positive views of Islamic law, which lead to sympathy for militants who claim their goal is to impose Sharia in Pakistan.

This book explores why Pakistanis think this way. It examines what factors drive their anti-Americanism. Why do they believe in Sharia? Why do they consider India to be Pakistan's greatest threat? Why do they suffer from a national sense of victimhood? Why do they subscribe to an "us versus them," an "Islam versus the West" narrative?

Before we go there—do these views really matter? If Pakistanis denounce violence, aren't we done here? Need we care about these wider narratives? The answer is yes. Militants thrive where their narratives find acceptance; they also find in such contexts fertile ground for recruitment. Citizens' narratives also affect their government's action against militant groups. In Pakistan, muted civilian demand for such action is at least one reason the government engaged in peace talks with the Pakistan Taliban in 2013–14 (the peace talks, in turn, also influenced the narrative, as I discuss in chapter 2).

TWO

Bound to Its Narrative

The Pakistani State and Terrorist Groups

Between the formation of the Pakistan Taliban in 2007 and the launch of the army's Zarb-e-Azb military operation against the group in June 2014, terrorist attacks claimed the lives of 23,700 civilians and security forces in Pakistan. In chapter 1, we saw what the Pakistani population had to say about the TTP. What did the Pakistani state have to say about the Taliban and related groups who waged an existential war against it, who attacked army installations, police academies, politicians, and ordinary citizens in parks and markets? To begin to understand Pakistanis' attitudes, it is instructive to look at the state's narrative on terrorism over the past decade.

STATE NARRATIVES ON TERROR:
THE BLAME GAME

On August 8, 2016, as the Quetta lawyer fraternity collected at a hospital to mourn and protest the killing of the president of the Baluchistan Bar Association earlier that morning, a suicide bomber struck the hospital's emergency room, killing more than seventy people. Nearly sixty of those who died that day were lawyers. This was a national tragedy, leaving Quetta, and Baluchistan, without what many called "an entire generation" of its lawyers. The target was clearly a community of educated, politically active people from Quetta. Both Jamaat-ul-Ahrar (JuA), a TTP splinter group, and ISIS separately claimed the attack.

But the Pakistani army and its civilian leadership framed the attack as an attempt to undermine the China Pakistan Economic Corridor, the pet project of the current Pakistan Muslim League–Nawaz (PML-N) government. The Baluchistan chief minister hinted at the involvement of India's intelligence agency, the Research and Analysis Wing (RAW), before the claims of responsibility by JuA and ISIS. The army chief Raheel Sharif also said the attack was an attempt to undermine the successes of Zarb-e-Azb, the army's operation against terrorists in Waziristan that began in 2014; by whom, he did not say.

The Pakistani state's explanations for terror usually vaguely allude to a "hidden hand" that wants to destabilize and sabotage Pakistan, to derail whatever "virtuous" venture Pakistan is involved in at the time—the China Pakistan Economic Corridor; peace talks with the Taliban, and so forth. At times the state leaves the culprit unidentified in the allusion to conspiracy after a terrorist attack despite claims of responsibility by a militant group. At other times, the civilian and military leadership—especially the latter—point the finger of blame at India and RAW. In one of its clearest statements, the army said, after a meeting of its senior-most commanders in May 2015, that RAW was "instigating terrorism" in Pakistan.

Opposition politicians and Islamists traffic in conspiracy theories, as well. After the attack at the All Saints Church in Peshawar killed more than eighty Christians in September 2013, Imran Khan, the star cricketer-turned-politician and leader of Pakistan's third-largest party, the Pakistan Tehreek-e-Insaf (PTI), said: "A conspiracy is being hatched to drag the country back to the ten-year-old morass."[1] He suggested the attack was conducted to derail soon-to-begin peace talks with the Pakistan Taliban.

Maulana Fazl-ur-Rehman, the loud, brash leader of Pakistan's second largest Islamist party (the Jamiat Ulema-e-Islam Fazl, JUI-F) used similar rhetoric in his response to the All Saints Church attack. He called the attack a "national calamity" but also said it was an attempt "to sabotage peace talks" with the Taliban. He said the attack "diminished Pakistan's image internationally and demanded the authorities to unmask the culprits behind the incident."[2]

If you lived in Pakistan, one could not blame you for not knowing who conducted the attack. Definitely not the Pakistan Taliban, you would think; after all, the political rhetoric said the attack was a conspiracy to derail peace talks with them. In fact, the attack was claimed by a faction of the Taliban, their spokesman saying: "We carried out the suicide bombings at [the] Peshawar church and will continue to strike foreigners and non-Muslims until drone attacks stop," adding that Christians "are the enemies of Islam, therefore we target them. We will continue our attacks on non-Muslims on Pakistani land."[3]

The state's typical response to a terror strike is confined to condemning the attack and repeating stiff platitudes that it will wipe out the menace of terrorism. In a statement following the All Saints church attack, Nawaz Sharif said: "The terrorists have no religion, and targeting innocent people is against the teachings of Islam and all religions."[4] Harmless enough, but this kind of banal statement misses the fact that the terrorists claim to espouse real Islamic ideology, call Sharif's government un-Islamic, and claim to want to impose Sharia on Pakistan. With Sharif's statement, the government missed the chance to counter the Taliban on each of these points.

More generally, the Pakistani state has never engaged in a clear conversation with its citizens about the terrorist groups targeting the country—explaining who they were, where they came from, what they say they want, and why they are wrong. It has offered no lessons in history, no clarity or guidance. The only time the Pakistani narrative on terror attacks has seen clarity is in the immediate aftermath of the Army Public School attack in Peshawar in December 2014 that killed more than 130 children. This attack shook Pakistan like nothing before (or since). The state named the Taliban as directly responsible for the attack and vowed to root the TTP and its sympathizers out. While part of this resolve has remained, signifying a real shift in direction, key aspects of it have washed away (this is discussed further in chapter 6).

Pakistani opposition politicians blamed U.S. drone strikes for terrorists' actions. At the height of the TTP insurgency and of U.S. drone strikes in 2012–13, Islamists as well as conservative opposition politicians like Imran Khan were obsessively focused on drones. Khan said drone strikes were the "root cause of militancy in Khyber Pakhtunkhwa and FATA."[5] Echoing the narrative of militant groups, he said there could be "no peace until drone strikes are stopped" and called for Pakistan to "pull itself out of the U.S.-led war on terror."[6] Though the government or army leadership did not indulge directly in this narrative, the state condemned strikes publicly while allegedly secretly approving them.

Does some of this sound familiar? It should. The Pakistani public's narratives described in the previous chapter—conspiracy theories and terrorists engaging in defensive actions—mirror those of the state. The only narrative of ordinary Pakistanis that does not follow directly from the state's narrative on terrorists is that of the Taliban engaging in a religious struggle to impose Islam—but the state plays an indirect role in that, too. It follows, as we shall see, from how the Pakistani state has ingrained in its citizens a vision of their country as an ideal Islamic state.

PEACE TALKS: GIVING THE MILITANTS A PLATFORM

The Pakistani state's peace talks with the TTP in 2013–14 reflect well not only the confused narrative on the group but also the government's policy toward it—of ambivalence at best, capitulation at worst. The PML-N party ran for the 2013 election on the promise of peace talks with the Pakistan Taliban at the height of the TTP insurgency.[7] After winning the May 2013 election with an impressive mandate, the government set the process of talks in motion soon after it came into power. It gave the Taliban the upper hand both in the talks and in framing the narrative around these talks. The government essentially did no homework; it set no agenda, no preconditions, and no goals for the talks. The militants took this as an opportunity for a free propaganda campaign, airing their views and articulating their narrative alarmingly well, saying that Pakistan's constitution did not have a "single element reflecting Islamic injunctions," and that Pakistan's "un-Islamic democratic system . . . of governance is the root of all evil."[8]

The government allowed the TTP to choose the members of the committee that would mediate between the government's representatives and the TTP's *shura* (governing body), instead of selecting this committee itself. The TTP selected two prominent Islamists—Maulana Sami-ul-Haq (head of the Jamiat Ulema-e-Islam Sami) and Jamaat-e-Islami's Ibrahim Khan (more on Islamist parties in chapter 5), and the militant Lal Masjid's fundamentalist cleric Abdul Aziz. All three were sympathetic to the Taliban.

Shahidullah Shahid, the TTP's spokesperson, said in interviews: "If talks are to be held [with the government] it would be only under Sharia. We have made this clear to the government committee. We are fighting for the enforcement of Sharia and we are holding talks for the same purpose."[9] Once talks began, he said: "The government has now accepted our reality; this is our victory."[10] It seemed as if the talks were being held on the Taliban's terms alone.

In addressing the question of Islam in Pakistan's constitution, the mediator Ibrahim Khan (of the Jamaat-e-Islami) said the constitution did have Islamic injunctions but implied they were not implemented properly—and that once they would be implemented, he would convince the TTP to accept the constitution.[11] His statement implied that the militants were in the right on their stance on the constitution.

The TTP and its sympathizers, thus, commanded the narrative while talks were being held. Their message was singular and delivered with stunning clarity. The government, meanwhile, fumbled, wrung its hands, waited for the Taliban's next move, and looked weak. It offered no alternative narrative to the Taliban and no direct narrative to the Pakistani people. It did not counter the Taliban's claim of wanting to enforce Sharia law in Pakistan, nor did it defend its alliance with the United States; it did not even counter the Taliban's arguments against the legitimacy of the Pakistani state.

In the end, the 2013–14 peace talks were suspended because the Taliban executed twenty-three Frontier Corps personnel in February 2014. When the TTP launched a particularly brazen attack on the Karachi airport in June that year, the government finally let go of the idea of talks, and the Pakistani army launched an offensive against the group in Waziristan, called operation Zarb-e-Azb (literally, the sharp strike; *Azb* also refers to the Prophet's sword).

There is a history to the state's behavior, as the rest of this chapter describes.

THE PAKISTAN NARRATIVE

To begin to understand the state's narrative and policy on the Pakistan Taliban, it is necessary to take a look at the ways in which the Pakistani state has come to define itself: at the state's reliance on Islam to define the Pakistani identity, and its defensive posture and paranoia vis-à-vis India. The Pakistan narrative, simply put, is that Pakistan is an Islamic state facing an existential threat from India. The other trends that define it—its military-civilian tensions and ultimate dominance of the military, its concession of space to Islamist parties, and its defensive view of itself in relation to the West—all follow from its two main narrative pillars, Islam and the Indian threat. These factors combined have, in turn, influenced the Pakistani state's relationship with, and narrative on, extremist groups.

It is not difficult to see how it suits a state paranoid of India to shift the blame of terrorism to it; how the affinity with Islam makes it difficult both to acknowledge that the terrorists are Muslims and to address and counter militant claims to Islamic ideology and law; and how that affinity also generates a narrative of Islam versus the West that, in turn, places the blame for terrorists' actions on Western policies. I'll spell these out in further detail, but first it is worth taking a look back to understand how Pakistan came to be defined this way.

The slogan "*Pakistan ka matlab kya, La ilaha IllAllah*" is heard in numerous places in Pakistan—in schools, at political rallies, at random junctures. "La ilaha illAllah" is part of the kalima, the declaration of faith in Islam, and the slogan literally translates to: "What does Pakistan mean? That there is one Allah." The intent of the statement is to convey that Pakistan is Islam; thus, by definition, an Islamic country.

This was not inevitable. Pakistan was created on August 14, 1947. Toward the end of British colonial rule on the Indian subcontinent, Muslim fears of a future as a political minority in a democratic united India led to demands for a separate state. After

failed negotiations between the Muslim League led by Mohammad Ali Jinnah and the Indian National Congress, it was decided
the state of Pakistan would be created from the Muslim-majority
provinces in the northwest of British India—Punjab, Sindh, Baluchistan, and the North West Frontier Province, which formed West
Pakistan—as well as the Muslim-majority area of Bengal to the
east, which formed East Pakistan.

At that point, the central—and open—question was what role
Islam would play in the new state created for the Muslims of the
Indian subcontinent. Pakistan, although predominantly Muslim,
was not necessarily intended (at least in the view of its founder Jinnah) to be an Islamic country. For Jinnah, Muslims in India were a
"nation" distinct from Hindus, and he had, therefore, advocated
for them to govern themselves. In his view, being Muslim was a
matter of identity, a form of ethno-cultural distinction. Hindus and
Muslims, he argued, "belong to two different civilizations. . . . To
yoke together two such nations under a single state, one as a nu-
merical minority and the other as a majority, must lead to growing
discontent."[12] This "two-nation theory" was Jinnah's justification
for Pakistan.

But the idea of Pakistan was somewhat paradoxical. It originated among a Muslim elite in Muslim minority areas of British
India. In those areas, the minority was threatened at the prospect
of lack of representation in an independent India but could not
create a new state where they lived; they had to create it in other,
Muslim-majority provinces. But "the elite in Muslim majority
areas were already in power and had little to fear from the Hindus."[13]
Second, the Muslims who were left behind—or who chose to stay
behind—in India also contradicted the idea that Indian Muslims
were one "nation."

Pakistan seems to have meant different things to different
people in the time leading up to its creation. Jinnah had in mind a
country where religion would not interfere in the affairs of the
state. He was liberal and personally secular. But even he sowed

confusion on the question of Islam's role in Pakistan. In the run-up to 1947 he said that Islam "was a complete code of life" and even promised Islamic government in Pakistan.[14] He and other Muslim League leaders seem to have used these statements to convince the Muslim-majority provinces that were to be part of Pakistan of the idea of the new state. As such they frequently invoked Islam and the notion of "Islam in danger."[15]

Other visionaries for Pakistan, such as the poet-philosopher Muhammad Iqbal—who came to be known as Allama Iqbal and was second in influence only to Jinnah—visualized Pakistan consistently as an Islamic country that would be a safe haven for Islam and where its practice could "continue unhindered."[16] In his presidential address to the All-India Muslim League in 1930, Iqbal spoke of a separate Muslim state as a place to protect "the life of Islam."[17]

Jinnah, for his part, walked back the explicit appeal to religion once independence was secured. In his most clear articulation of his secular vision for Pakistan, he said during his August 11, 1947 address to the Constituent Assembly in Karachi: "You are free. You are free to go to your temples; you are free to go to your mosques or to any other place of worship in this state of Pakistan. You may belong to any religion or caste or creed—that has nothing to do with the business of the state."[18]

Jinnah never actually used the word *secular* in that speech, but proponents of a secular and liberal Pakistan frequently invoke his words of that day. But given his differing statements on the issue, both sides of the Islamic-secular debate in Pakistan call on Jinnah's words to defend their own claims, though the entirety of his statements and his personal beliefs make it clear that his vision for Pakistan was one of a modern Muslim democracy—almost certainly not an Islamic state. Jinnah died of illness a year after partition, in 1948, a blow to the new nation, and he left the fundamentals of Pakistan unresolved.

This ambiguity on the ultimate purpose of the newly founded state left a lasting legacy of differences between secular and Islamist elements in Pakistan. Perhaps the issue was destined to be fraught—here was a country created for Muslims, but the role of religion in the new state was never clearly defined. It is not surprising, then, that some thought that the logical conclusion was an Islamic state. The slope from Muslim nation to Islamic state is a slippery one.

In the new Pakistani state, there were political imperatives to rely on Islam—each of West Pakistan's four provinces and East Pakistan had different ethnic-cultural identities, and the Pakistani state used religion for nation-building. Initially, to get the different ethnicities—the Punjabis, the Sindhis, the Baluchis, the Pashtuns, and the Bengalis, each corresponding to a separate province in the new nation—on board with the idea of a new state, Jinnah had promised a loose federal structure with autonomy for the provinces. In his Lahore resolution speech in March 1940, Jinnah stated that the "constituent units [of a new state] shall be autonomous and sovereign."[19] But the Muslim Legislators' Convention changed the wording of the resolution in 1946 to a more centralized framework for the new state. Shortly after independence, in a speech aired on Radio Pakistan from Dhaka in March 1948, Jinnah denounced provincialism: "I want you to be on your guard against this poison of provincialism that our enemies wish to inject into our State."[20] The result was a suppression of ethnic and provincial identities in favor of the common religious identity.

The new state also used a common language for unity. Urdu, Pakistan's national language, was, in fact, the language of migrants to West Pakistan, some of whom had originally been involved in the demand for Pakistan and then became its initial rulers. Liaquat Ali Khan, Jinnah's close associate and Pakistan's first prime minister, was one such migrant from Uttar Pradesh (UP) to the new West Pakistan. The fact that these initial leaders were not from the areas they came to rule meant that their connection to their constituents was weak. Their need for legitimacy led the nascent Pakistani state to rely on Islam.

Perhaps the biggest reason to rely on Islam was that Pakistan felt it needed religion to define its citizenry as different from that of India; despite Jinnah's argument of two nations, Pakistan shared a history and cultural heritage with India. Islam became the state's tool of choice to continually defend the need for Pakistan and to differentiate Pakistan culturally and nationally from India. The two pillars of the state narrative, then, reinforce each other. Pakistan is anti-India because of its association with Islam, and an Islamic state to assert its opposition to India.

Islam has also proven useful for Pakistan's military, which relies on it to justify war with India and to sanction violence in the name of jihad. The army's purpose is nationalist, but the religious framing provides it legitimacy. Its evocation of religion is direct: its motto is *"Iman, Taqwa, Jihad-fi-sibilillah"* (faith, piety, holy war).[21] The continued specter of conflict with India keeps Pakistan in a permanent militarized state, and it sustains the military's status as the country's most powerful institution. Because of this strength, the army has ruled Pakistan for more than half of its seven decades. Pakistan's military has controlled the country's internal and external security policy through regimes both military and civilian, and that control has defined the state's relationship with extremism.

Pakistan has been committed to its Islamic narrative and ideology during both military and civilian governments, through leaders personally religious and secular. The secular Ayub Khan, a military man, president of Pakistan from 1958 to 1969, referred to religion as the "only foundation for national unity" and called Pakistan a "fortress of Islam."[22]

Reliance on Islam has also meant a strategic use of Islamists by the state. These Islamists, including the Jamaat-e-Islami party and its leader Syed Abul A'la Maududi, initially opposed partition on the ground that geographical boundaries were antithetical to the concept of a universal Muslim ummah. They had been skeptical of the secular Jinnah and other League leaders, and once these

Islamists joined the new country, they realized they had the power to become a potent pressure force on the state despite their poor performance in elections. Mainstream Islamists became a significant vehicle for radicalization in Pakistan through their role in the Afghan jihad; they have also blocked progressive reform and, more recently, efforts to counter extremism.

If there is one event that cemented Pakistan's Islamic, anti-India narrative, it was the loss of East Pakistan in 1971. This furthered Pakistan's internal insecurity as well as its insecurity vis-à-vis India. East Pakistan seceded because of resentment at being improperly represented and for ethno-linguistic and political reasons—despite the religious unifier with West Pakistan. Bangladesh's independence convinced the weakened Pakistani state that Pakistan's ethnic diversity was a threat and that cultivation of a singular identity based on the only unifier it perceived—Islam—was the way forward. So it doubled down on Islam, despite the fact that for the years immediately after 1971 Pakistan was ruled by the personally liberal Zulfikar Ali Bhutto. Bhutto defined his governing philosophy as "Islamic socialism," proclaiming: "Islam is our faith. Democracy is our polity. Socialism is our economy."[23] He also linked Pakistan with the Islamic world after 1971.

That India intervened in helping East Pakistan secede rendered Pakistan perennially paranoid of India's intentions post-1971. This plays out in Pakistan's suspicions of Indian involvement in the Baluch insurgency and underlies the state pointing to India for wanting to destabilize it through terror.

Pakistan's reliance on Islam has asserted itself in multiple ways—in its laws and education, discussed later—and in its sense of its place in the world and its foreign policy. Stephen Cohen characterizes the Pakistani establishment's philosophy as Islamic nationalism, a "worldview that stems from nationalist and foreign policy motives," that is anti-India, distrustful of the United States, anti-Israel, and based on solidarity with Muslim countries.[24]

Pakistan seeks to become a formidable Islamic power. However, in the day-to-day functioning of the Pakistani state you could miss its focus on religion—the bureaucracy, politicians, and army carry out their tasks in an almost secular way, in keeping with the vestiges of colonial British rule. The Pakistani state is practical; it seeks to be modern, especially in the sense of economic advancement. It is keen to create strategic partnerships with advanced countries in the West, and with China. Pakistan's closest ally, in fact, is China—not a Muslim country or an Islamic state. Pakistan sees itself—or wants to be seen—as an integral part of the modern world, a successful country of strategic importance.

Thus you could be fooled about the importance of its religious narrative. But that narrative underlies everything of significance and has become immutable. It is not driven by an ideological desire for religion, however; it is for the reasons I've sketched out, both strategic and political, that the Pakistani state is convinced of the usefulness of its master narrative; indeed of its indispensability.

But in service to this narrative, the Pakistani state facilitated the creation of jihadists in the 1980s and 1990s, and, more recently, has made poor choices—looking the other way from militants, legitimizing them—that have emboldened terrorists. That is, both the creation of terrorists in the country and the spread of radical views in the population can be tied back to the master narrative. Yet the Pakistani state is still convinced it can walk the line between its master narrative and radicalism.

THE AFGHAN JIHAD AND THE CREATION
OF JIHADISTS

From 1977 to 1988 Pakistan was ruled by a military dictator, General Muhammad Zia-ul-Haq. He was austere, a consummate British-trained army man, brutal and widely disliked. He ruled over Pakistan with an iron hand. He was personally devout, but he used

Islam ruthlessly for political and strategic ends. He believed that without Islam "Pakistan would fail."[25] His regime introduced and mainstreamed the concept and the terminology of the "Pakistan ideology," that Pakistan was created for Islam. As described in chapter 4, with the help of the Jamaat-e-Islami party, he used this concept to transform educational curricula. Under the guise of Islamization, he also changed parts of Pakistan's legal system, rendering some laws discriminatory at best and draconian at worst.

But Zia's most damning legacy came from his role in the (U.S.- and Saudi-funded and supported) anti-Soviet Afghan jihad. For all his hardline beliefs and policies, Zia was pro-America, and his term was a high point of U.S.-Pakistan relations. He joined the U.S.-Saudi alliance not to support the fight against communism but to acquire "strategic depth" for Pakistan in Afghanistan that would boost its power with regard to India. The argument was that a friendly government in Afghanistan would boost Pakistan's regional standing and counter the Indian threat on its east with an ally to its west. That the strategic decision to counter India in this way was taken during army rule is not a surprise.

The cause was strategic, but the methods used were not. The Afghan resistance against the Soviet occupation was framed as a religious jihad, its fighters called mujahideen. They were armed as much with ideology as with guns; the armed resistance was conflated deliberately with Islam. This suited Zia. Steve Coll argues that "a war fought on Islamic principles could . . . help Zia shore up a political base at home and deflect appeals to Pashtun nationalism."[26] Thus the same imperatives that led Pakistan to rely on Islam—the need for political legitimacy and fear of internal fractures—led it to use Islam in this external war. In fact both Islam and countering India—Pakistan's two narrative pillars— played a role in driving Pakistan into the Afghan jihad.

Both America and Saudi Arabia funded the jihad, and America provided arms and technical advice. Pakistan (and its Inter-Services

Intelligence, the ISI) trained the Afghan fighters as well as Pakistani volunteers who joined the jihad. The training was both ideological and military, and it was conducted in new madrassas in Pakistan and in existing ones repurposed for the jihad.

A mainstream Islamist party, the Jamiat Ulema-e-Islam (JUI), ran many of these madrassas. The JUI's rural madrassas were already the "main conduit for the dissemination of Wahhabi Islam" in Pakistan in the 1970s.[27] These madrassas multiplied in number during the 1980s and, through them, the JUI became a major supplier of mujahideen for the Afghan jihad.

The military's ISI conducted the trainings and the management of the Afghan mujahideen. Coll argues that America left the choice of picking political winners among the Afghan resistance to Pakistan, and that Pakistan chose the more radical fighters over Pashtun leaders because the jihadists were better fighters (in its view) and because the Pashtun fighters were "likely to stir up Pashtun nationalism inside Pakistani territory,"[28] and would have been threatening to an internally insecure Pakistan.

Many of the well-known militant-linked madrassas in Pakistan today—the one at Lal Masjid, the Binoria madrassa in Karachi, and Lashkar-e-Taiba's Dawat-ul-Irshad—were established during this time. These madrassas were mostly Sunni, and the ones supported by Saudi Arabia were Wahhabi.

The immediate result of the Afghan jihad was a dramatic increase in money, arms, and hardline religious ideology in Pakistan; the latter two far outlasted the Soviet withdrawal, as did the jihadi groups created during this time, the madrassas, and the Pakistani men who were trained in them. The worst outcome of the whole affair in some ways was the normalization of the concept of jihad as a tool in modern Pakistan. The success of this strategy in Afghanistan led the ISI to use it next to the east, in Kashmir, against its biggest foe: India.

KASHMIRI JIHADISTS AND THE STATE

Some of the Pakistani jihadi groups that fought the Soviets—the Harkat-ul-Mujahideen (HuM) and Harkat-ul-Jihad-al-Islami (HuJI)—turned their focus toward the Kashmir cause once the Soviets withdrew. It is understood that Pakistan's Inter-Services Intelligence directed them that way, to aid what had begun as an organic resistance in Kashmir against Indian rule in 1989.[29] Here was a second example of the Pakistani army using Islam for war, in this case against its existential threat, India—another decision in service to its narrative.

Since then, the ISI has reportedly given cover and support to jihadist groups fighting in Kashmir—particularly to Lashkar-e-Taiba, Jaish-e-Mohammad, and Harkat-ul-Mujahideen. In some cases these groups have acted as proxies for the ISI; in others, they have acted more independently. The army's support has meant a financial backing, but these groups also generate money through donations. They are able to function and organize in the heart of Punjab. These groups also have ties with Islamists. Hafiz Saeed, the head of Lashkar-e-Taiba (and its political and charitable arm, Jamaat-ud-Dawa), is a former member of the Jamaat-e-Islami.

In response to foreign pressure to take action against these groups, the Pakistani state has engaged in purposefully negligible prosecution toward them. This is why Hafiz Saeed can give public speeches and openly hold large rallies with a $10 million American bounty on him. It is also why Kashmiri jihadist groups are able to rename and reconstitute themselves after they have been banned. During those times, the charity wings of these militant groups, such as the LeT's Jamaat-ud-Dawa (JuD), function as acceptable fronts for the groups. JuD was ostensibly officially banned in 2015, but it continues to function freely.

When one of these Kashmir-focused militant groups is held responsible by India (or the West) for a large-scale attack, like LeT for the Mumbai attacks in 2008 or JeM for the Pathankot air base attack in 2016, any punitive action against the group, its leader, and its facilities tends to be short-lived and largely symbolic. When the furor dies down, things go back to the way they were. Hafiz Saeed has been detained multiple times—after September 11 in 2001, and after attacks in India in 2006 and 2008—only to be released after a few months with the claim that there were no grounds to keep him detained. Similarly, JeM's Masood Azhar was taken into protective custody after September 11 and later released.

These jihadi groups do not target Pakistani civilians or the state directly; their enemy is clearly India. But the concept of jihad is unwieldy, and the rhetoric of these groups is not limited to liberating Kashmir. They are anti-Israel, anti-America, and anti-West. They say their ultimate goal is to impose Sharia in South Asia, and they talk of support for a global jihad. This is explicit in their pronouncements, as in the Jamaat-ud-Dawa's manifesto, titled "Why Are We Waging Jihad": "Is there any place in this world today where Muslims are not suffering? Are there not cries for help from the downtrodden Muslim men, women and children in Indian Kashmir, the Philippines, Chechnya, China, Russia, Bosnia among other places, all pleading to be saved from their torments?"[30]

The blurring of lines across jihadist groups is not limited to rhetoric; they sometimes provide sanctuary to members of other groups, and their own fighters "migrate" across groups. According to the U.S. State Department, a top al Qaeda lieutenant was discovered at a LeT safe house in 2002.[31] And Coll reported that LeT fighters joined the fight with the Afghan Taliban in the mid-2000s: "Some of its [JuD's] younger volunteers wanted to join the fight with the Taliban in Western Pakistan and Afghanistan . . . and so Jamaat [ud-Dawa] had evolved an internal H.R. policy by which these young men would turn in their Jamaat identity cards and go West 'on their own time,' much as think tanks allow policy scholars to take leaves of absence to advise political campaigns."[32] Thus these groups pose a direct security risk to Pakistan, but Pakistan's India-obsessed army fails to recognize that—it feels they can be contained, or that their strategic use is worth the risk.

The Pakistani state has allowed these Kashmiri militant groups to function as social-political-militant entities. They openly provide charity and extensive social services, as described in chapter 1. This helps them win over Pakistanis' hearts and minds. In 2016, Pakistani newspapers reported the existence of an illegal JuD Sharia court in Lahore, running parallel justice to the state. The government seemed to have no knowledge of it. JuD denied it was running a court and said it was engaged only in arbitration. But the person who first reported the story to the media—the "defendant" in a case—showed he had, in fact, received a summons to the court.

These militant groups are also able to freely publish and distribute their propaganda. JuD and LeT run a slate of magazines in multiple languages—Urdu, English, and Arabic—with large circulations. LeT also runs a magazine for students and one for women in addition to publishing dozens of booklets and maintaining websites in Urdu, Arabic, and English.[33]

THE CREATION OF THE PAKISTAN TALIBAN

Two wars—the Afghan jihad of the 1980s and the U.S. invasion of Afghanistan after 9/11—provide necessary context to understand the formation of the Pakistan Taliban. Some of the Pakistani fighters who fought the Afghan jihad returned home to lawless tribal areas, a neglectful government, and no rehabilitation. They subsequently turned their attention and their jihad inward to Pakistan. One of these men was Sufi Muhammad. He was a former Jamaat-e-Islami leader who quit the Jamaat in 1981, "citing irreparable ideological differences," essentially on the use of violence— Jamaat-e-Islami is committed to nonviolence—and joined the Afghan jihad.[34] Upon his return to Pakistan, he formed the Tehrik-e-Nifaz-Shariat-Mohammadi (TNSM) in 1989. The goal of that group was to impose Sharia in Dir. His TNSM was a precursor of the Tehrik-e-Taliban Pakistan. Fazlullah, the current leader of the Pakistan Taliban, is Sufi Muhammad's son-in-law.

Once the United States declared war in Afghanistan in 2001, groups like Sufi Muhammad's TNSM used the narrative of resistance to the U.S. "occupation" and the Pakistani government's alliance with America to gain strength in the lawless tribal areas. They introduced courts offering quick justice and began conducting terror attacks against the Pakistani state. Mullah Fazlullah propagated jihad against the U.S. "invaders" in Afghanistan in daily FM radio broadcasts in 2006 and 2007 and declared fatwas on girls' schools, calling them "centers of all evil"; these accorded him the title Mullah Radio.[35]

The state did not recognize these precursors of the Pakistan Taliban as an existential threat, and given the state's complicity in the Afghan jihad, this was not a surprise. The narrative was that they were "our brothers" and could be contained.

Between 2005 and 2007, under General Pervez Musharraf's government, the army engaged in three successive peace deals with the precursors of the TTP. Each of these failed, but to the public they legitimized the militants and their cause. The deals also helped the militants logistically, giving them space to regroup and expand. After a 2005 deal with the militant Baitullah Mehsud, the army's General Safdar Hussain said that Mehsud was "not a rebel but a patriotic citizen and soldier" of Pakistan.[36] But Haji Omar (a militant commander) and Baitullah did not back down from their insurgency and stated publicly that they would be continuing their jihad against the U.S.-led coalition in Afghanistan.

The summer of 2007 and the events at Islamabad's Lal Masjid (Red Mosque) proved to be a turning point for these groups. The brothers at the militant Lal Masjid—Abdul Aziz and Abdul Rashid Ghazi—were openly inspired by Osama bin Laden. Their incendiary rhetoric was well known, as was the fact that they trained students who joined the various militant groups operating in the northwest in the 2000s—as they had for the Afghan jihad in the 1980s. Abdul Aziz's wife ran Lal Masjid's women's wing, Jamia Hafsa. In 2007, students from Jamia Hafsa started going around Islamabad with sticks, trying to enforce Sharia—raiding massage parlors, video shops, hotels. Musharraf launched an operation against the madrassa, and the entire sordid encounter played out on television. Fifty seminary students were killed, along with Ghazi. The action proved to be too much for the public's appetite, and too late. Abdul Aziz threatened Musharraf with retaliatory attacks, and "publicly thanked Allah for giving Fazlullah and Sufi Muhammad the power to enforce Sharia."[37] The state lost the war of public opinion and of narrative, especially in the newly free media environment that Musharraf had set up. Soon after this, the Pakistan Taliban was officially born, and the spike in terror was unmistakable (see figure 2-1).

The state continued to shuffle its feet on the militants. Baitullah and Fazlullah were declared "patriotic" in a confidential media briefing in 2008.[38] In early 2009, the TTP took over the Swat valley in Khyber Pakhtunkhwa, then known as the North West Frontier Province (NWFP). The federal government (by that point headed by President Asif Ali Zardari) and the provincial government

FIGURE 2-1. **Fatalities in Terrorist Violence in Pakistan, 2003–16**

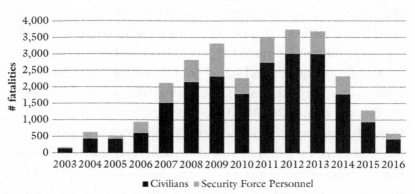

Source: South Asia Terrorism Portal (www.satp.org/satporgtp/countries/pakistan/database/casualties.htm).

(headed by the secular Awami National Party) then signed a peace deal with the TTP through which Sharia was imposed in Swat in an effort to end the violence. Government officials said this was a positive development for Swat, that it would "bring swift and fair justice" to an area that had lacked it. The chief minister of NWFP said: "There was a vacuum . . . in the legal system. The people demanded this and they deserve it."[39] In October 2012, the TTP attacked Malala Yousafzai, a fifteen-year-old activist for girls' schooling in Swat.

The state's successive peace deals and talks with the Pakistan Taliban, and the lack of willingness to recognize the existential threat they posed to the state, followed from its role in the Afghan jihad. Because jihadists had been of strategic use to the Pakistani state in Afghanistan and in Kashmir, because the state had used them in service to its master narrative, and because they were "their brothers"—Muslims—even when the jihadists turned against the Pakistani state, the state thought they could be contained. This, in turn, drove its narrative on the TTP and the public's image of these groups.

THE CIVILIAN-MILITARY EQUATION AND A PERSISTING NARRATIVE

The Pakistan military, the most powerful institution in the country whether in power or not, considers it a vital duty "to defend not only the territorial integrity of the country but also its ideological frontiers," as per the army's official website. For the military, Islam forms this ideological frontier. On its official website, the army states its motto: "*Iman, taqwa, jihad fi-sibilillah.*"[40] *Iman* is faith, *taqwa* is piety and fear of God, and *jihad* means to fight for God. In explaining what it means by *jihad*, it references the Quranic statement that it is the duty of Muslims to "fight in the cause of God those who fight you and be not aggressors. God loveth not those who are aggressors."[41] The army is clear that it considers India the aggressor.

On its website, the army points to a rethink of its strategic doctrine in 1976, which it says had, until then, been influenced by the West. The shift, it says, was in light of "our geostrategic realities and operational environment."[42] The revised doctrine introduced "core issues of Quranic concepts of warfare, regulated by laws like Jihad," but also (among other things) encouraged "negotiations for honourable peace and that enemies need not be permanent."[43]

Pakistan's army pitched the wars it fought against India as jihad. Newspaper advertisements asking for donations for the National Defence Fund in the 1971 war repeatedly referenced jihad; as an example, one read: "Jihad means total commitment."[44] When the conventional wars against India failed, Pakistan realized that its smaller size and weakness relative to India warranted a different strategy (this likely underlies the army's "rethink")—thus it invested in developing nuclear capabilities, its "Islamic bomb." Prime Minister Zulfikar Ali Bhutto began Pakistan's nuclear development effort as a defensive move against India, with the goal to make Pakistan a formidable Islamic power. The army says Pakistan's acquisition of nuclear weapons "established a strategic balance in the region, 'striking terror into the hearts of the enemy' as enjoined by the Holy Quran."[45] Even the nuclear bomb, a strategic decision, is portrayed as a religious imperative by the state.

Nawaz Sharif, the current prime minister, was in his second term as prime minister when Pakistan first tested its nuclear capabilities at Chagai in Baluchistan in 1998. His rhetoric around his decision to test the bomb is instructive. "Today, we have evened the score with India," he said. "India is an expansionist country. We constantly pointed towards this fact but the major powers did not pay any attention to this and continued to believe in false pronouncements made by Indian rulers."[46] He was clear that the decision to test the bomb was a response to Indian aggression, a question of Pakistan's national pride and honor, and a matter of preserving and defending its sovereignty in the face of Western pressure not to test. While his narrative was largely a nationalist one, he, too, gave it a religious veneer by naming the day of the tests, May 28, *Youm-e-takbir,* the day of reaffirming faith.

Pakistan's sense of fundamental insecurity and weakness relative to its larger, stronger rival and its defeat on a traditional military footing led to other decisions beyond nuclear development to level the playing field; it led the army to embrace the policy of the Afghan jihad—to acquire influence in Afghanistan given fears of Indian encirclement—and later the covert Kashmir jihad. The army still believes the threat of Kashmiri jihadists, its strategic "assets," is what keeps an aggressive India at bay.

The civilian-military balance in Pakistan has consistently tipped to the side of the military through the decades. And because the military has controlled Pakistan's security policy, its policies have become immutable. Some reasons for the military's dominance are deeply rooted because of the Indian threat, which is, thus, in the military's interest to perpetuate indefinitely. Because the military has intervened in Pakistani politics and overthrown democratic regimes continually, when civilian politicians rule, they do so with a sense of paranoia, as if in survival mode, putting out fires and being extractive in their limited time in power. This leads to a self-reinforcing, cyclical military dominance. The civilians' incompetence and corruption, in turn, does not inspire confidence from the country's citizens, and tips the balance back in favor of the military.

Since the launch of its Zarb-e-Azb operation in 2014 and, indeed, in a few years leading up to it, the military's policy has clearly differentiated between those militants it believes pose a direct threat to the Pakistani state (the TTP) and those it believes are of strategic use to it (the Afghan Taliban and LeT)—the "bad Taliban" versus the "good Taliban." Until 2014, Pakistani politicians obfuscated on the "bad Taliban," engaging in some of the rhetoric laid out at the beginning of the chapter, and argued that talks were the way to go. The military seems to have been waiting for them to come around and, after the Karachi airport attack in June 2014, began action.

Recently the civilians seem to have evolved more on the issue than the military. There seems to be, in recent months, a new recognition by the country's democratic government that the military's continuing "good Taliban–bad Taliban" distinction is foolhardy and runs counter to Pakistan's own interests, but the army still seems unwilling to let it go. Consider the following incident.

In October 2016, a front page article by a prominent journalist in *Dawn*, Pakistan's premier English daily, recounted an unprecedented showdown between Shahbaz Sharif, chief minister of Punjab and brother of Nawaz Sharif, and the head of the Inter-Services Intelligence (ISI), in which the civilians asked the ISI to end the protection it gives to Kashmiri and Afghan jihadists.[47] The matter blew up immediately. The prime minister's office—which likely leaked the story—issued multiple breathless denials of the story, and after a meeting between Nawaz Sharif and the army chief General Sharif, the interior minister placed a travel ban on the journalist and announced an inquiry into the matter. The military's Inter-Services Public Relations said the leaks that led to the story were "a threat to national security." There were two matters at stake: the projection of a shift in the civil-military power equation over security matters and the reference to an internal acknowledgment of the ISI's cover for jihadists. Both irked the military greatly, and its reaction was intense—although most of it could be inferred only from the actions of the PM office and interior ministry. This underscores how difficult a shift of power in the military-civilian equation on security is going to be, and how reluctant the army is to openly acknowledge its dual policy toward militant groups, let alone change it. To be fair, there is doubt that the civilians are up to the task of handling security policy, but it is also clear that the military is not ready to let it go.

THREE

Pakistan's Legal Islamization

THE GOVERNOR AND HIS KILLER

On January 4, 2011, Salmaan Taseer, the governor of Punjab, Pakistan's most populous and prosperous province, was murdered in broad daylight in Islamabad by one of his elite-force security guards. As the governor returned to his car after having lunch, the killer, Mumtaz Qadri, recited "*La Ilaha IllAllah, Muhammad-ur-Rasool Allah*," the Islamic declaration of faith (There is no God but Allah, and Muhammad is his Prophet) before he shot Taseer twenty-seven times. Qadri surrendered immediately.

Taseer, a successful businessman and politician known for his liberal and Westernized views and lifestyle had, in the weeks before his murder, championed the case of Asia Bibi, a poor Christian woman sentenced to death on charges of blasphemy in November 2010. A group of Muslim women in her village had accused Asia Bibi of insulting the Prophet after they had an argument over drinking water she had brought to them (they argued it was "un-clean" because she was Christian). Taseer stood out among Paki-stani politicians in his vocal opposition to the country's blasphemy law, which he called "man-made" and a "black law" in television interviews as he campaigned aggressively for its reform.[1] On De-cember 31, days before his death, he wrote on Twitter: "I was under huge pressure 2 [to] cow down b4 [before] rightist pressure on blasphemy. Refused. Even if I'm the last man standing."

Qadri pled guilty to the murder and declared he had killed Taseer because his support for Asia Bibi and his stance against the blasphemy law made him an apostate.[2] The killer called himself a "slave of the Prophet."[3] The night of the murder, there appeared to be equal amounts of sympathy for the murderer and for his victim across Pakistan, perhaps more for the former.[4] On Pakistani television, anchors argued that it was understandable, if not justi-fiable, that Taseer had been killed, given his support for amending the blasphemy law. Many did not condemn the killing. Even those who did refused to refer to Taseer as a *shaheed*, or martyr. On Facebook, fan pages for Qadri cropped up, and thousands changed their profile pictures to an image of his face.

Five hundred religious clerics, leaders of Jamaat-e-Ahl-e-Sunnat, a leading Barelvi religious party, issued a warning to followers tell-ing them to stay away from Taseer's funeral the next day: "No Muslim should attend the funeral or even try to pray for Salmaan Taseer or even express any kind of regret or sympathy over the incident."[5] On the other hand they said: "We pay rich tributes and salute the bravery, valour and faith of Mumtaz Qadri."[6] Islamists, including Fazl-ur-Rehman and Jamaat-e-Islami's Munawwar Has-san, said that anyone who defended a blasphemer or spoke out against the blasphemy law was a blasphemer himself.

Taseer's indulgent, partying lifestyle was well known. For many conservatives, that, combined with his stance against the blasphemy law, made him a bad Muslim. For the most extreme of the lot, this meant he was *wajib-ul-qatl*, worthy of being killed. As Taseer was buried in Lahore, his killer was cheered at a court appearance in Islamabad and was showered with flower petals by lawyers.

The government indicated quickly and clearly after Taseer's assassination that it would not pursue reform of the blasphemy law. The polarization of Pakistani society that the killing brought into relief was stark and unprecedented. Pakistan's liberals mourned Taseer online, on blogs, on Twitter, and in the op-ed pages of English-language newspapers. All the major political parties condemned the attack. On the other side, the killing united otherwise divided religious parties and groups, who "found common cause on blasphemy" and a mission in defending Qadri.[7] And the common man seemed to agree with them. The day after the killing, the *New York Times* interviewed a twenty-five-year-old shop owner who had recently completed college, and he said: "We are Muslims and nobody can compromise on the dignity of the Prophet. Salmaan Taseer crossed the limits."[8] Many stayed silent; the fear, understandable, that the assassination evoked in those who sympathized with the governor's cause was formidable. In the end, those who hailed Qadri the killer as a hero were louder than those who mourned Governor Taseer, his victim.

It turned out that Qadri was a follower of the Islamic organization Dawat-e-Islami, which purports to purify society from "the evils"—alcohol, music, movies, gambling, immodesty—though it does not promote violence.[9] Dawat-e-Islami is a relatively popular Barelvi movement in Pakistan; its followers are easily identifiable in their green turbans in major cities. Qadri was sentenced to death in October 2011. His case eventually ended up in Pakistan's Supreme Court in October 2015, where a landmark judgment upheld his death sentence. A plea for clemency to Pakistan's president was denied in February 2016, and Qadri was hanged on February 29, 2016, five years after he had killed Taseer. It is hard to overstate the courage of the Supreme Court and the government in taking this stance, given that popular support for Qadri had remained strong over the five years since the murder.

More than 100,000 mourners turned up at Qadri's funeral in Rawalpindi's Liaquat Bagh on March 1, 2016. A lawyer who attended the funeral was quoted in the *Wall Street Journal*: "We condemn terrorism. What Mumtaz Qadri did had no malice. He was in love with the Prophet. He had no bad intention."[10] Another man, a twenty-two-year-old engineering student who had traveled 130 miles to attend the funeral, said in an interview: "The government has no shame, it has no honor. It has done this to please its masters in America. How can an Islamic state execute a man who loves the Prophet so much?"[11]

A mosque named after Qadri in Rawalpindi that was built during his lifetime remains, and a large shrine has been built where he is buried near Islamabad. Hundreds visit his grave every day. The man who leads prayers at the Mumtaz Qadri mosque and who oversaw its construction was quoted in Pakistan's *Dawn* newspaper: "My faith is not that strong. Otherwise I and every other Muslim would also do what Mumtaz Qadri did."[12]

On March 27, just weeks after his funeral, thousands attended the *chehlum* held to commemorate forty days of Qadri's death at Liaquat Bagh in Rawalpindi. Thousands of Barelvi mullahs marched from that event on to the Parliament and Presidency in Islamabad, paralyzing the capital and costing millions of rupees in damage, leading the government to call the army to restore order. They sat at D-chowk on Constitution Avenue for four days, demanding the "unconditional release of all Sunni clerics and leaders booked on various charges, including terrorism and murder; the recognition of Mumtaz Qadri as a martyr and the conversion of his Adiala Jail cell into a national heritage site; assurances that blasphemy laws will not be amended; and the removal of Ahmadis and other non-Muslims who occupy key posts" in the government.[13] The government negotiated with the protesting mullahs on these demands, and they ended their sit-in when the government assured them of no amendments to the blasphemy laws and no clemency to anyone convicted under them.[14] The mullahs won the round.

For Qadri's many supporters in Pakistan, he is the hero, the martyr, who was brave enough to do the right thing. For them he was a defender of the Prophet and an exemplary Muslim who killed a man who was *wajib-ul-qatl*, worthy of being killed, for his stance on blasphemy. But to you and me, it is obvious that Qadri was a fanatic and a terrorist.

Pakistan's blasphemy laws as they currently stand were instituted as amendments to the country's penal code between 1980 and 1986. The change in laws coincided with a dramatic increase in accusations of blasphemy (a shift that is hard to argue is not causal given its magnitude). Before 1986, only fourteen blasphemy cases were recorded in Pakistan. But between 1986 and 2010, according to Pakistan's *Dawn* newspaper, an estimated 1,274 blasphemy cases were recorded.[15] At least fifty-two of the accused were killed extra-judicially before the end of their trials.

What do Pakistan's blasphemy laws look like, and where did they come from? The story begins with the country's legal Islamization, starting from its birth.

A GRADUAL LEGAL ISLAMIZATION

According to Pakistan scholar Farzana Shaikh, post-partition, the majority of Pakistan's new leaders, even the most personally secular ones, seemed to envision an "Islamically informed constitutional order" for Pakistan—although without an understanding of or any agreement on specifics.[16] Still, their conception of Islam's role in Pakistan was Muslim-modernist, based on "Islamic ethical and social concerns" rather than strict Islamic law. Many of these early elites had also been leaders of the Pakistan movement and were secular "Muslim nationalists," like Jinnah. Islamist parties and the ulema, however, who had initially opposed the idea of Pakistan, wanted to implement Islamic law in the new country.

Pakistan's legal Islamization began with the Objectives Resolution of 1949, the twelve guiding principles for its future constitution. The resolution was a balanced, if vague, document (see appendix A for the full text). Islam was mentioned in three clauses, which dealt with divine sovereignty; the importance of the democratic, social, and ethical principles of Islam; and enabling Muslims to live their lives according to Islam. The resolution also guaranteed the equal rights of religious minorities, and their freedom of expression and of worship, though this was "subject to law and public morality."

In the debate on the resolution in the Constituent Assembly, Muslims supported it but non-Muslims opposed it, pointing out that the "enabling" clause focused on Muslims alone as opposed to all religions (they argued the latter would have been consistent with Jinnah's vision). Still, the resolution passed.

Defending the enabling clause, Pakistan's first prime minister, Liaquat Ali Khan, said that the state was:

> not to play the part of a neutral observer, wherein Muslims may be merely free to profess and practice their religion, because such an attitude would be a very negation of the ideals which prompted the demand for Pakistan . . . the state will create such conditions as are conducive to the building up of a truly Islamic society, which means that the state will have to play a positive part in this effort.[17]

Overall, the resolution struck a tolerant chord, treating minorities with respect and assuring them of full rights. But the enabling clause also set up the country for its legal Islamization. The Jamaat-e-Islami heralded the Objectives Resolution as a victory for Islam and for the Jamaat, and as a step in favor of an Islamic constitution.

After the Objectives Resolution passed, the Jamaat-e-Islami and its head Syed Abul A'la Maududi upped the pressure on Pakistan's leaders and demanded Sharia and an Islamic state. In November 1952 the Jamaat organized a "constitution week," demanding Islamic provisions in Pakistan's constitution. It suited the Muslim League, on the other hand, to keep the role of Islam vague.[18] But Vali Nasr argues that "the Jamaat's propaganda and maneuvering and Maududi's untiring campaign for Islamisation foiled the attempts both of Muslim Leaguers . . . to extricate Islam from politics and of the government to manipulate Islam for its own ends."[19]

Pakistan officially became the Islamic Republic of Pakistan in its 1956 constitution. The Objectives Resolution formed the preamble. The 1956 constitution also mandated that only a Muslim could be president (the head of state), thus institutionalizing explicit discrimination against non-Muslims in the country's top leadership, but there was no restriction (yet) on the religion of the prime minister (the head of government).

Perhaps the most important Islamic feature of the 1956 constitution was the "repugnancy" clause (article 198), which stated that "no law shall be enacted which is repugnant to the Injunctions of Islam as laid down in the Holy Quran and Sunnah, hereinafter referred to as Injunctions of Islam, and existing law shall be brought into conformity with such Injunctions."[20] The constitution stated that this clause would be implemented via a commission that would advise the federal and provincial legislatures on the issue. In Pakistan's current constitution this role is fulfilled by the Council of Islamic Ideology.

The "enabling clause" from the Objectives Resolution was expanded upon in the 1956 constitution; it stated that steps would be taken to enable the Muslims of Pakistan individually and collectively to order their lives in accordance with the Quran and Sunnah, the Prophet's teachings. It went on to say that the state would endeavor to provide facilities where Muslims would be enabled to understand the meaning of life according to the Quran and Sunnah; make the teaching of the Quran compulsory; and promote unity and the observance of Islamic moral standards. The constitution also stated there would be an organization set up for Islamic research "to assist in the reconstruction of Muslim society on a truly Islamic basis."[21]

Making the teaching of the Quran compulsory and promoting the observance of Islamic moral standards goes beyond "enabling" Muslims to live their lives according to Islam, to an imposition of religion and religious values. Yet at that point the constitution was still vague—what were these "Islamic moral standards"?—about how it would do so.

The 1956 constitution guaranteed the rights of all religions. Article 18 stated that citizens had the freedom to profess, practice, and propagate any religion and the right to establish, maintain, and manage religious institutions. This, sadly, was to change in the 1970s and 1980s.

When the military chief Ayub Khan imposed martial law in 1958, the 1956 constitution was abrogated. Ayub, who was secular and a modernizer, instituted Pakistan's second constitution in 1962. This second constitution decreed that Pakistan was no longer an Islamic state; it became the "Republic of Pakistan." Ayub also removed the direct reference to the Quran and Sunnah in the repugnancy clause, which was reworded to say, simply, that no law should be repugnant to Islam, making the reference to religion vague.

Ayub's two bold moves did not last long. Islamists agitated, and he was forced to reinstate a direct reference to the Quran and Sunnah via the first constitutional amendment of 1963.[22] Via the same amendment, Pakistan once again became an Islamic Republic.

This illustrates the path of Pakistan's legal Islamization. It was all but impossible to walk back any references to Islam once they were made constitutionally. Otherwise the 1962 constitution followed the 1956 constitution on Islam. The wording of the enabling clause was more or less the same as in 1956, but stated that the teaching of Islamiat (Islamic studies) was to be compulsory for Muslims in addition to the Quran.

The 1973 constitution, which is the current constitution of Pakistan, declared Islam the state religion. It also stated that the president and prime minister were both to be Muslim, cutting off non-Muslims from the two highest leadership positions in the country. In both these ways it took a firmer stance in favor of Islam than Pakistan's previous two constitutions. This almost surely had to do with the insecurity Pakistan felt after the secession of Bangladesh in 1971. Under this pressure, Prime Minister Zulfikar Ali Bhutto, while personally secular, spoke of "re-Islamising" Pakistan, and even promised to institute Sharia in nine years.

The enabling and repugnancy clauses in 1973 mirrored those in the 1956 constitution. The advisory body that was to review laws to determine repugnancy to the Quran and Sunnah—a commission in the 1956 constitution—would be called the Council of Islamic Ideology.

The constitution guaranteed freedom of religion "subject to law, public order and morality," and freedom of speech "subject to any reasonable restrictions imposed by law in the interest of the glory of Islam or the integrity, security or defense of Pakistan or any part thereof, friendly relations with foreign States, public order, decency or morality, or in relation to contempt of court, or incitement to an offense"[23]—a long, albeit vague, list. Freedom of speech was to be curtailed more explicitly later.

The 1973 constitution guaranteed that members of a particular religion would not have to study another religion: "No person attending any educational institution shall be required to receive religious instruction, or take part in any religious ceremony, or attend religious worship, if such instruction, ceremony or worship relates to a religion other than his own."[24] This law, as we will see in chapter 4, has been violated by Pakistan's official curriculum.

Until 1973, then, the Pakistani constitution promised to adhere to Islam and promised the future Islamization of the legal system through the repugnancy clause. It also foreshadowed, through the enabling clause, the Islamization of society, making teaching of the Quran and Islamiat compulsory and promoting the observance of Islamic moral standards.

There are two main takeaways from Pakistan's constitutional development until 1973. First, the 1956 constitution laid the groundwork for the final, 1973 constitution. Many of the key elements in reference to Islam, such as repugnancy, remained; Ayub's attempts to walk them back in 1962 failed. On certain dimensions— the enabling clause, for instance—there was a gradual increase in Islamization. Second, the focus on Islam in the constitution signified implicit discrimination against non-Muslims, but the only explicit discrimination was barring them from the highest offices of prime minister and president. Overall, the Pakistani constitution made an effort to be fair. That was to change after 1974. And while the Islamization in the constitution until 1973 set the foundation for what was to come next, things could have gone the other way; the law could have remained tolerant and fair.

LEGALIZING EXTREMISM

Two sets of clauses, both instituted into Pakistan's penal code under Zia's regime in the 1980s—the anti-Ahmadi legislation and the blasphemy laws—criminalized perceived infractions and offenses to Islam, with draconian punishments in the case of the blasphemy law. As I will show next, these laws set the stage for state-sanctioned exclusion and extremism, and encouraged vigilante violence against minorities.

Anti-Ahmadi Laws

Ahmadis are followers of Mirza Ghulam Ahmad, a nineteenth-century Indian religious leader who claimed to be the Messiah in fulfillment of an Islamic prophecy. Most Muslims reject his claim and consider it to violate the core principle of Islam that Muhammad is the final Prophet. But Ahmadis consider themselves Muslim. For them, Ahmad was "subordinate in status to Prophet Muhammad; he came to illuminate and reform Islam, as predicted by Prophet Muhammad."[25]

In 1953, the Islamist groups Jamaat-e-Islami and Majlis-e-Ahrar led riots against Ahmadis, demanding they be declared non-Muslim. Hundreds died. In response, the government cracked down on the rioting Islamists, and the Governor General Malik Ghulam Muhammad dismissed Prime Minister Khawaja Nazimuddin and his cabinet. For the next twenty years, there was no major agitation against the Ahmadis. But in 1974, there was an altercation between the student wing of the Jamaat-e-Islami, called the Islami-Jamiat-e-Tulaba (IJT), and Ahmadis in the Ahmadi spiritual headquarters of Rabwah. After that, the Islamists once again launched a hundred-day campaign, called the Tehrik-e-Khatm-e-Nabuwwat (the Movement for the Finality of Prophethood), to have Ahmadis declared non-Muslim.

Zulfikar Bhutto tried in vain to sidestep the "Ahmadi question." But he was still on the defensive after 1971, insecure about his own secular credentials and eager to appease and co-opt the Islamists. Saudi Arabia's king also apparently pressured him on the issue. Bhutto ultimately caved and let the Ahmadi issue go to a vote in parliament; the Ahmadis were designated as non-Muslims on September 7, 1974, via the second amendment to the 1973 constitution. The constitution now—without naming

Ahmadis directly—defined a non-Muslim as someone who did not believe in the absolute finality of Prophet Muhammad, or someone who recognized a prophet or religious reformer after Muhammad.[26] As a result, Ahmadis could no longer call themselves Muslim. They also could no longer become prime minister or president.

In 1985, the military dictator Muhammad Zia-ul-Haq expanded on this by explicitly naming Ahmadis as well as other religious groups as non-Muslim.[27] A year earlier, he had codified limits to the words and actions of Ahmadis via clauses 298-B and 298-C of the penal code.[28] It became illegal for Ahmadis to "directly or indirectly pose as Muslim." They could no longer call themselves Muslims or their places of worship mosques; they could not recite the Azan, the Muslim call for prayer; and could not refer to Mirza Ghulam Ahmad with an Islamic honorific. They also could not "in any manner whatsoever outrage the religious feelings of Muslims." These "offenses" carried a punishment of up to three years.

With these new laws, Ahmadis lost all freedom to profess and practice their religion. As an example, they could not use Islamic terminology such as the Kalima, the core tenet of Islam ("There is no God but Allah, and Muhammad is his Prophet") anywhere: not on wedding invitations, not during funeral prayers, not on gravestones, not on a wall hanging at their place of work, not on their own clothing. Many were arrested and charged for displaying the Kalima.

Ahmadis appealed 298-B and 298-C, but the government saw to it that Sharia benches instituted by Zia (more on these later) heard the case.[29] Because non-Muslim lawyers, and thus Ahmadis, could not argue in the Sharia courts, the Ahmadis' case was at a disadvantage. The Sharia courts ruled against them. In 1993, the Supreme Court also denied their appeal.

The government defended its case with incendiary rhetoric. In the hearing before the Federal Shariat court on clauses 298-B and 298-C, the deputy attorney general said: "death is the penalty for those who do not believe in the finality of Prophethood and in Islamic countries it is a heinous crime. It is not necessary that the government should take action, but on the contrary any Muslim can take the law in his own hands."[30] In a speech on December 7, 1984, Zia said: "there is no place for infidels in Pakistan . . . if a man's honor is attacked he does not even hesitate from committing murder . . . if someone is put against him [the Prophet Muhammad], what should be the reaction of the people?"[31] Both statements promoted vigilantism. In a message to the International Khatm-e-Nabuwwat conference in London in August 1985, Zia said: "we will, InshaAllah, persevere in our effort to ensure that the cancer of Qadianism [Qadiani is another name for Ahmadi] is exterminated."[32]

In the three years immediately after the anti-Ahmadi law was instituted in the penal code—between 1984 and 1987—at least twelve Ahmadis, professionals and community leaders, were reported murdered.[33] Of course, the two large-scale incidents of rioting and bloodshed in 1953 and 1974 occurred before any constitutional law or penal code changes had taken place. What increased after 1974, and especially after 1984, were deliberate, dispersed acts of violence by individuals and groups directed against members of the Ahmadi sect. These could call upon the law as justification.

In recent years terrorists have targeted the group, as well. In October 2005, gunmen attacked Ahmadis at an Ahmadi mosque in Mandi Bahauddin in Punjab, killing eight worshippers. The perpetrators were never caught. In the largest attack on the group, two Ahmadi mosques in different parts of Lahore were attacked by at least six terrorists on May 28, 2010. Ninety-six Ahmadis were killed, and more than 100 wounded. The Punjab branch of the Pakistan Taliban claimed responsibility for the attacks. Eyewitnesses said the attackers shouted the slogan *"Khatm-e-Nabuwwat Zinda Baad,"* meaning "Long live the finality of the Prophet."[34] The constitution has handed this justification to terrorists.

Three days after the mosque attacks, on May 31, gunmen attacked the Intensive Care Unit at Jinnah Hospital in Lahore, where the injured victims were being treated. Twelve more people, mostly hospital staff and police officers, died in that attack.

After the attacks, the media did not refer to the Ahmadis as Muslims. They would be breaking Pakistani law by doing so. Reporters and commentators did not even refer "to the Ahmadis by name, preferring the phrase 'minority community.'"[35] Even in Pakistan's liberal English-language newspapers, including *Dawn*, the attacked mosques were referred to as "places of worship." Pakistani society now finds itself unable to treat Ahmadis as fellow Muslims or as equal citizens. The othering of the Ahmadis is ingrained in society via Pakistan's constitution.

Indignities, small and large, confront Ahmadis beyond the threat of violence. On their passport and national identity card applications, Pakistani Muslims have to sign the following statement: "I consider Mirza Ghulam Ahmad an impostor prophet. And also consider his followers, whether belonging to the Lahori or Qadiani group, to be non-Muslims."[36] If Ahmadis sign it, they are declaring their own prophet an impostor. If they don't, they have to declare themselves non-Muslim.

That the military dictator Zia-ul-Haq instituted the laws against Ahmadis was no coincidence. No Pakistani leader to date has relied on Islam as heavily as Zia, or used it as forcefully or cynically. He framed a 1984 referendum to extend his rule as a referendum on Islam. He asked Pakistanis:

Do you endorse the process initiated by General Muhammad Zia-ul-Haq, the President of Pakistan, for bringing the laws of Pakistan in conformity with the injunctions of Islam as laid down in the Holy Quran and Sunnah of the Holy Prophet (PBUH) and for the preservation of the Islamic ideology of Pakistan, for the continuation and consolidation of that process, and for the smooth and orderly transfer of power to the elected representatives of the people?[37]

It was claimed that 98.5 percent of those who voted said yes.

Zia doubled down on Islam to derive strength due to his lack of democratic legitimacy. His referendum wording is evidence of that. His personal religiosity played a role in his reliance on Islam, but he also used religion politically, strategically, and militarily—not only ideologically—by courting Islamists and by engaging in the Afghan jihad.

The second change Zia made in an effort to "shariatize" Pakistan's legal system, after his anti-Ahmadi legislation, was in its blasphemy laws.

Blasphemy Laws

Pakistan's penal code was written in 1860 by the subcontinent's British colonizers. In 1980, Zia added a clause to the penal code that criminalized derogatory remarks against companions of the Prophet and other religious figures.[38] Such remarks were to be punished with a prison term of up to three years.

Clauses 295-B and 295-C, which Zia inserted in 1982 and 1986, respectively, into the penal code, form the harsh, regressive core of Pakistan's blasphemy law. Clause 295-B deals with defiling the Quran: "Whoever willfully defiles, damages or desecrates a copy of the Holy Qur'an or of an extract therefrom or uses it in any derogatory manner or for any unlawful purpose shall be punishable with imprisonment for life."[39] Clause 295-C criminalizes derogatory remarks against the Prophet: "Whoever by words, either spoken or written, or by visible representation or by any imputation, innuendo, or insinuation, directly or indirectly, defiles the sacred name of the Holy Prophet Muhammad (peace be upon him) shall be punished with death, or imprisonment for life, and shall also be liable to fine."[40]

Previously, clauses 295 and 295-A (the latter added by the British in 1927) dealt with offenses toward any religion and carried a maximum sentence of a ten-year prison term. But Zia's clauses 295-B and 295-C focused only on blasphemy toward Islam, and equated an offensive act or speech with a capital offense.

What kind of words exactly are these that can be punished by death? The law is anything but specific. Innuendos, insinuations, indirect words, anything construed by someone as derogatory can lead to death. Who is to decide what is derogatory? It's all subjective. The law is, thus, easy to misuse. There are documented cases where it has been used to settle personal grudges. And what a weapon it is. The severity of the punishment means that the life of anyone accused, whether wrongly or not, is ruined. A mere accusation of blasphemy can lead to violence against the accused, justified in the eyes of the vigilantes by clauses 295-B and 295-C.

With one swoop, Zia's blasphemy laws negated freedom of speech, discouraged open differences in religious opinion, and made it dangerous to question or debate interpretations of Islam. Even questioning the blasphemy law or calling for its reform is now construed as blasphemy. No wonder, then, that the law has been remarkably resistant to reform.

Let's go back to the case of Asia Bibi. After the government noticed her case, President Asif Ali Zardari formed a parliamentary committee to review the blasphemy laws. Sherry Rehman, a member of the Pakistan People's Party (PPP) on the committee, introduced a private bill in parliament in December 2010 to amend the law. Her bill aimed to prevent wrongful use of the law and sought to reduce punishments for blasphemy, removing the death penalty—specifically, to make the maximum penalty ten years in prison; to make only those actions or words liable to blasphemy that were undertaken or said "maliciously, deliberately and intentionally"; to make false accusations of blasphemy punishable; to make "advocacy of religious hatred" punishable; and to change the level at which blasphemy cases were tried, so that as many cases were referred to the high court level as possible.[41]

Two prominent politicians spoke out in support of Asia Bibi and in favor of reforming the law: Punjab Governor Salmaan Taseer and Religious Minorities Minister Shahbaz Bhatti, a Christian. Bhatti was a member of the parliamentary committee formed to review the law and had said that Asia Bibi should be pardoned.

Taseer was killed in January 2011. In February, the Pakistan People's Party withdrew the bill to reform the law. Sherry Rehman was called an apostate by clerics and was under virtual lockdown at her home in Karachi for months because of threats to her life. In March 2011, Bhatti was killed in Islamabad. At Bhatti's assassination site, fliers made reference to the parliamentary committee "in support of the blasphemers" that was led by "a Christian infidel, a cursed one, Shahbaz Bhatti."[42] No wonder advocates for blasphemy law reform are silenced and fear for their lives.

According to the National Commission for Justice and Peace (NCJP), 1,335 Pakistanis have been accused of blasphemy between 1987 and 2014: 633 Muslims, 494 Ahmadis, 187 Christians, and twenty-one Hindus. The majority of these cases were lodged for desecration of the Quran; fewer for blasphemy against the Prophet.[43] In 2014 alone, the NCJP noted that 105 people were charged with blasphemy: eleven Ahmadis, seven Christians, five Hindus, and eighty-two Muslims.[44] In 2016, the U.S. Commission on International Religious Freedom noted nearly forty individuals were either sentenced to death or serving life sentences for blasphemy in Pakistan, although no death sentence for blasphemy has yet been carried out.

Because fellow citizens lodge blasphemy cases, and because the number of cases has increased dramatically—from virtually nonexistent pre-1986 to, on average, fifty documented cases a year—it is difficult to argue that the blasphemy law did not have a causal impact on Pakistanis, either affecting their attitudes directly or exposing already intolerant attitudes.

Ahmadis are particularly vulnerable to the blasphemy law. The Ahmadi belief in the prophethood of Mirza Ghulam Ahmad is considered by some to defile the name of the Prophet Muhammad and, thus, blasphemous and punishable by death. Ahmadis have been charged for blasphemy every year since the introduction of the blasphemy laws; more than a third of those accused of blasphemy between 1987 and 2014 were Ahmadis, although they form a tiny percentage of the population.

In October 2015 Pakistan's Supreme Court issued a historic judgment when it upheld Taseer's killer Mumtaz Qadri's death sentence, giving a flicker of hope on blasphemy law reform. It made clear that calling for reform of the blasphemy law is not equal to blasphemy: "It goes without saying that seeking improvement of a manmade law in respect of a religious matter for better or proper enforcement of such law does not *ipso facto* amount to criticizing the religious aspect of such law."[45]

The Court was clear in its stance against blasphemy. Yet it did not advocate for repeal of the law, only for safeguards against its misuse: "Any call for reform of the law regarding the offense of blasphemy ought not to be mistaken as a call for doing away with that law and it ought to be understood as a call for introducing adequate safeguards against malicious application or use of that law by motivated persons."[46] It condemned false accusations of blasphemy and said that it was the duty of the Pakistani state to ensure that no one falsely accused of blasphemy had to face trial.

It also issued a strong warning against vigilantism:

If the asserted religious motivation of the appellant (Qadri) for the murder committed by him by taking the law in his own hands is to be accepted as a valid mitigating circumstance in this case then a door shall become open for religious vigilantism which may deal a mortal blow to the rule of law in this country where divergent religious interpretations abound and tolerance stands depleted to an alarming level.[47]

That Zia transformed Pakistan's legal system in this way is in some ways particular to him and to Pakistan's non-democratic history, but it also goes back to the political imperatives of the Pakistani state to rely on Islam. The country's legal Islamization until 1973, especially the repugnancy and enabling clauses, and Bhutto's declaration of Ahmadis as non-Muslim in 1974, helped set up the groundwork for Zia's changes. Zia likely would have found it harder to make his amendments without that foundation.

Not content with the strictly advisory role of the Council of Islamic Ideology (CII), the constitutionally mandated body to enforce the repugnancy clause, Zia also created "Shariat benches" in each of the provincial high courts in 1979 to rule on the repugnancy of laws to the Quran and Sunnah.[48] In 1980, Zia also established a Federal Shariat Court,[49] which could issue mandatory rulings. Given its advisory role, the Council of Islamic Ideology effectively became subordinate to the Federal Shariat Court.

These religio-legal institutions—the Shariat benches, the Federal Shariat Court, the CII—are now overlapping, confusing, and largely ineffective. But they have succeeded in elevating the legal position of the ulema in Pakistan. At key points, these institutions have spoken out in favor of Zia-era legislation, against repeal or reform of those laws and against current attempts at progressive reform in Pakistan (as an example, they opposed recent legislation to prevent violence against women). As mentioned, the Shariat benches upheld the anti-Ahmadi laws; since only Muslims could argue in Shariat courts, Ahmadis could not represent themselves in these courts.

Zia also enforced Hudood laws, which further "shariatized" Pakistan—enforcing Sharia-like legislation—that in particular served as a blow to the status of women. The laws criminalized adultery and introduced draconian punishments such as stoning to death for adultery and chopping off hands for theft. If their own state instituted these kinds of punishments, should it be any wonder that certain Pakistanis do not balk as much when a militant group does the same? Though no one has ever been stoned to death by the state for adultery in Pakistan—the burden of evidence, four male witnesses, is too high and practically impossible to achieve—the very fact that such a punishment exists on paper is enough. That the state can police morality also legitimizes actions taken by vigilantes and militant groups when they do the same at movie theaters and video shops and massage parlors. And because their own state has taken steps toward Islamic law (in some instances, a draconian interpretation of it), the Pakistani public is sympathetic toward that ideological goal when it is claimed by militant groups—though the militants' version of Sharia incorporates tribal customs and by no means is pure Islamic law.

I want to be clear that legal Islamization does not—in itself, in any way—imply a necessary rise in extremism or sympathy toward extremists. But Pakistan's anti-Ahmadi laws and its blasphemy laws are discriminatory—violating principles of equality and freedom of speech and of religion, and the right to practice religion—and this discrimination not only engenders intolerance but also violence. Because the laws institutionalize a violent response by the state to speech or actions that may be construed as blasphemous while leaving what constitutes blasphemy open to interpretation, they pave the way for vigilante violence.

The laws also affect how ordinary citizens respond to militant violence. When militant groups target minorities that have been otherized by the state because of their faith or their religious views and militants claim it is because of these very reasons that they targeted them—the targeted minorities do not always generate sympathy from ordinary Pakistanis.

When Pakistanis are asked in interviews how they think religious minorities fare in their country, the typical answer is that they are doing all right; respondents will point to the written protection for minority rights in the constitution, to Jinnah's intentions, to the fact that Muslims are also targeted by militants—and they will also be quick to point to how badly they think Muslims are doing in India and in the West. Unless otherwise noted, the following data I discuss are from the Pew 2011 poll on religion.[50] Seventy-five percent of Pakistani Muslims say people of other religions are very free to practice their faith in Pakistan. Only 6 percent of respondents believe the blasphemy laws unfairly target minorities—yet the fact is that Pakistan's blasphemy laws disproportionately target the marginalized and religious minorities.

Pakistanis approve of the blasphemy laws. Seventy-five percent of Pew respondents said that blasphemy laws are "necessary to protect Islam" in Pakistan. But they believe that people of any religion should not be able to offend other religions. In the 2015 Pew poll, 67 percent say the government should be able to prevent people from making statements that are offensive to minority groups. Yet the Pakistani government implements this only for statements construed as offensive against Islam.

As mentioned in chapter 1, 84 percent of respondents favored making Sharia the official law of the land in Pakistan, although a majority of these respondents (64 percent) say Sharia should apply to Muslims only. For Pakistani Muslims, it seems clear that the country was created as a place for Muslims to practice Islam, but at the same time they believe all people should be able to practice their own religion freely in Pakistan (in the 2015 Pew poll, 84 percent say this was very important, the same percentage that says this in the United States!). Yet Pakistan's anti-Ahmadi laws violate this principle.

Only 41 percent of respondents believe Pakistan's current laws closely follow Sharia. Of those who say the country's laws do not follow Sharia, 91 percent say this is a bad thing. And their conception of what Pakistan's laws should look like for Muslims is strict. In the 2015 Pew survey, 78 percent said that Pakistan's laws should strictly follow the teachings of the Quran (as opposed to laws that follow the values and principles of Islam but do not strictly follow Quranic teachings), paralleling the strict wording of Pakistan's repugnancy clause. Sixty-one percent of Pakistani Muslims view Sharia as inflexible, saying it has only one single interpretation.

Pakistanis buy into the country's legal Islamization and believe in Sharia, which suggests that—to counter the appeal of militant groups who use the rhetoric of Sharia—the Pakistani state needs to show differences between valid Islamic laws and the invalid conception of Islamic law used by militant groups. But the state loses the ground to do that when the anti-Ahmadi and blasphemy laws derive from a debatable conception of Islamic law themselves.

Pakistanis have an unrealistic sense of the lives of minorities in the country, believing in a freedom of religion that is in actuality denied by law to certain groups—in particular, the Ahmadis. Yet some of the exclusionary nature of Pakistan's laws has seeped through into attitudes. Ninety-two percent of Pakistani Pew respondents said that Islam is the one true faith leading to eternal life in heaven, and 75 percent favor the death penalty for converts who leave Islam, parallel to the state-instituted punishment for blasphemy.

During the last week of December 2016, the Pakistani city of Lahore truly felt like a city of the world. One could see Christmas decorations in many parts of the city. Pakistan's current Pakistan Muslim League-Nawaz (PML-N) government, in its rhetoric and its symbolic gestures, was invoking "Quaid's Pakistan" (Jinnah is referred to as Quaid-e-Azam, or Great Leader, by Pakistanis) and the equal rights of minorities. It launched a Christmas peace train that month, as well.

Yet on January 4, 2017, on the fifth anniversary of Taseer's killing, Lahore's traffic came to a standstill for hours, blocked by

"*Islam bachao*" (Save Islam) rallies held by Tehreek Labaik ya Rasool Allah, an umbrella organization of Barelvi fundamentalist groups that shot to prominence after it organized the pro-Qadri D-chowk sit-in of March 2016. Separately, on January 4, the Punjab police arrested over 100 clerics in Lahore for attempting to celebrate Taseer's killing. The Islam bachao rally was not covered prominently in the media—presumably to prevent its message from getting undue publicity—in itself a positive development. Ashraf Asif Jalali, the head of the Tehreek, issued a rambling press release at the Lahore Press Club before the rally. He said they planned to protest a range of issues, including blasphemy, America's support of Israel at the expense of Palestinians, the suffering of Muslims around the world—in Syria, Myanmar, Kashmir—and the dangers to Pakistan's ideology from foreign interference.

Jalali called for one of Taseer's sons to be taken in by the state for blasphemy, saying his remarks (arguing against the blasphemy law in defending his father) were an insult to Muslims everywhere, and the state should arrest him so that vigilantes did not take the law into their own hands. He said the fundamental idea that Islam is the only true religion was being washed away in deference to minorities in Pakistan and that its education system was under threat from foreign interference. He referred to a recent report by the U.S. Commission on International Religious Freedom (US-CIRF) that recommended Pakistani schools stop teaching students an exclusionary version of Islam. Jalali warned against this sort of "ideological interference" and called it a direct attack on Islam; he reiterated that Islam was the only true religion and teaching schoolchildren otherwise was extremely dangerous.

Why are Pakistani schools of significance? What are students learning and how does that affect their attitudes? We discuss Pakistan's education system next, in chapter 4.

FOUR

An Ideological Education

Soon after he took power, General Muhammad Zia-ul-Haq made Pakistan Studies (a course on the history and geography of the country) compulsory for all students working toward a degree, even engineering and medicine. This was in 1981, the same year the University Grants Commission issued a new guiding directive to authors of Pakistan Studies textbooks: the books were "to demonstrate that the basis of Pakistan is not to be founded in racial, linguistic, or geographical factors, but, rather, in the shared experience of a common religion. To get students to know and appreciate the Ideology of Pakistan, and to popularize it with slogans. To guide students towards the ultimate goal of Pakistan— the creation of a completely Islamized State."[1]

Zia used the Pakistan Studies textbooks as the means to impart his view of Pakistan to the country's youngest minds. In this, he found a partner in the Jamaat-e-Islami (JI), the scholarly Islamist party with whom the term "Pakistan ideology" likely originated.

The 1951 manifesto of the Jamaat-e-Islami contains the terminology: "Nobody should indulge in anything repugnant to the Ideology of Pakistan. Any effort directed towards turning this country into a secular state or implanting herein any foreign ideology amounts to an attack on the very existence of Pakistan."[2] The Jamaat believed Islam needed to be a fundamental part of the public school curriculum and had pushed for this since the 1950s. The Jamaat's leader, Syed Abul A'la Maududi, wanted a Pakistan where "every subject would become Islamiat."[3]

Prior to 1977, no textbook contained any mention of the "Pakistan ideology." But after that, the construct became the starting point and the central premise of high school Pakistan Studies texts. The description of Pakistan Studies textbooks that follows is based on my reading and analysis of textbooks from the mid-1990s to today, from all four provinces. The books state, quite simply, that the Pakistan ideology *is* Islam, and begin by describing the five pillars of Islam—*shahada* (the declaration of faith), *namaz* (prayer), *zakat* (charity), *hajj* (pilgrimage), and fasting—that, together, form the basis of Islamic practice. But this material in the textbooks violates the constitutional provision that non-Muslims do not need to study Islam. In addition, defining the Pakistani identity solely in the form of Islam excludes non-Muslims from that identity.

Islam features heavily in the books—in one thin volume, the Punjab textbook from 2002, I counted 255 mentions of Islam. The Jamaat's influence is palpable: according to Pervez Hoodbhoy and A. H. Nayyar, Pakistan's history textbooks use "much the same idiom, and the same concepts of Islamic state and of politics in Islam, as the Jamaat-e-Islami."[4] In discussing Islam, the textbooks also emphasize individual and social Islamic values, which are broad and universal. The textbooks assert that religion defines Pakistan's role in the world positively: "As an Islamic country, Pakistan stands for international cooperation and peace. Islam teaches us peace and amity and discourages aggression. Although Islam allows to raise arms in self-defense yet it strictly prohibits domination or persecution of people through military force. Pakistan has been taking necessary steps to promote international brotherhood and peace on the basis of these Islamic principles."[5] There is little wrong with this particular set of statements—note the argument that one can take up arms but only in self-defense. Yet in the repeated references to Islam the books establish it as a given that, in Pakistan, religion permeates politics, policy, and society; and they entirely ignore aspects of the country's history and culture (and the parts of its population) that are non-Islamic.

THE "ENEMY" AND JIHAD

Justifying the creation of Pakistan is a key purpose of the books—thus it follows that, after "ideology," the books move on to the "making" of Pakistan. They posit Pakistan's creation as inevitable given that Hindus and Muslims were "two nations," fundamentally different "in their religious ideas, their way of living and collective thinking" and unable to intermingle with each other during their entire history as coresidents of the subcontinent.[6] The reality is that the two did coexist peacefully, despite times of friction; in the end it was politics in the years preceding 1947 above all—an iterative back and forth between the Muslim League and the Indian National Congress that ultimately did not work out—that drove the Muslims to arrive at their two-nation theory and to partition. And though the textbooks detail the events in the years leading up to partition, they do so with the premise that the two-nation theory was immutable, and that partition was, thus, inevitable. That premise is flawed because it suggests divisions and insurmountable enmity with people of different religions.

The textbooks' rendering of history is decidedly one-sided. Leading to independence, Muslims are described as the wronged party, the victims of conspiracies by the British and Hindus (the "evil collusion between the Congress [party] and the British" is an example of the kind of language used).[7] The Muslims of the subcontinent are depicted as good, their intentions always sincere; the other side is described as the opposite. The language used is noteworthy for its starkness and lack of nuance. Hindus are at times described as "evil"; at others, "cunning," and sometimes simply as the "enemy."

The books go further. In early chapters, they extol warfare that occurred pre-partition against armies of other religions, and describe it in religious terms, as jihad. As an example, one textbook states that Syed Ahmad Shaheed Barelvi (an important religious, political, and military figure from the early nineteenth century) preached "jihad because it was not possible to get freedom from evil force without armed struggle."[8] The "evil force" in question is the Sikhs—an alarming characterization, especially when coupled with the promotion of armed warfare in the name of religion.

At times the books mention jihad directly in the discussion on Islam and describe it in both its connotations (as an armed struggle and as an individual, internal struggle):

Besides Hajj (the annual pilgrimage to Mecca), Jihad also has great significance. Jihad means that financial and physical sacrifice which is made for the protection and promotion of Islam. Jihad not only means to fight against the enemies of Islam but also to make a struggle for the promotion and enforcement of Islamic teachings, keeping one's desires and wants under the orders of Allah and uttering words of truth before a tyrant ruler.[9]

The textbooks also invoke jihad to describe Pakistan's wars with India post-partition. Recounting the 1965 war, one textbook states: "The Armed Forces of Pakistan, filled with the spirit of Jihad, forced an enemy many times bigger than it to face a humiliated defeat"[10] (Pakistan did not actually win the 1965 war; the assertion of victory is factually incorrect).

High school Pakistan Studies textbooks begin with the state's two narrative pillars loaded up-front, purposefully, to foster in students a nationalism based on Islam and derived in opposition to India. It is noteworthy that jihad is mentioned up-front and at least partially in its armed connotation, although the mentions of jihad are nowhere near as constant as the focus on religion and on the "enemy" next door, and as described later, they have recently been toned down further as part of a curriculum reform.

PAKISTAN'S EDUCATIONAL LANDSCAPE

The previous examples are based on grade 9 and 10 textbooks that prepare students toward the matriculation (matric) exam, a board examination required for graduating from government high schools, and private high schools that follow the government curriculum, across Pakistan. Let's take a quick look at Pakistan's educational landscape, so we can place the reach of these textbooks in context. According to Pakistan's National Education Census of 2005 (the country's only such census of educational institutions to date), 2.1 million students were enrolled in matric grades 9 and 10 in that year. Of these, 1.5 million were in public schools and 600,000 in private schools. (Think of these as low- to medium-tuition schools that at the high school level follow the government curriculum; their students must take the matric exam to be granted a degree.) A parallel, British system runs at the high school level as well, with select groups of students in elite private schools preparing for the Cambridge-administered O-level board exams. These schools account for a tiny percentage of enrollment; only 3,658 students in Pakistan were enrolled in O-levels in 2005, just 0.2 percent of the matric total (although the influence of this elite class of Pakistanis goes far beyond its numbers, and these numbers have also been rising quickly).

Completed education levels for Pakistanis are available only from the 1998 census (see appendix B, table B-1), so they are dated (Pakistan is this year undertaking its first census after nineteen years). According to the 1998 census, only 52 percent of the population has attended school beyond elementary school, and 30 percent has completed matric (or more). This is changing. Current gross enrollment rates are 91 percent, 56 percent, and 59 percent at the primary (grades 1 to 5), middle (grades 6 to 8), and secondary levels (grades 9 to 10), respectively.[11] For now, there are two things worth noting. A significant proportion of the population doesn't make it to high school, and the vast majority of the students who do go through the government-administered matric system.

Madrassas, or religious seminaries, are a third type of education system in Pakistan. They were linked in the wake of 9/11 with extremism, raising a wave of alarm internationally about the number of children enrolled in Pakistani madrassas. Initially, enrollment numbers were pegged at a million or more (across education levels). A team of academic economists—Tahir Andrabi, Jishnu Das, and Asim Khwaja—debunked the numbers on madrassa enrollment and prevalence in a set of papers. Using the 1998 census, they showed that only 0.3 percent of all Pakistani children were enrolled across grade levels in madrassas; between the ages of five and nineteen, madrassa enrollment accounted for 0.7 percent of all enrolled children.[12] Using the Pakistan Integrated Household Survey, the authors showed that public schools account for 73 percent, and private schools 26 percent, of all enrollment; madrassas make up less than 1 percent of overall enrollment. There are reasons these madrassa enrollment numbers may be an underestimate. They are self-reported and based on those who report madrassas as the primary place of enrollment. There are also important variations in madrassa enrollment across regions—we will further discuss madrassas and the key question of what is taught in these seminaries in the following chapter—but it is worth understanding at this point that the government curriculum is almost universal for school-going children in Pakistan.

WHO WRITES THE TEXTBOOKS?

Historically, the provinces were responsible for writing their own textbooks in Pakistan in accordance with the national curriculum, which was developed by the federal curriculum wing associated with the federal ministry of education. Within each province, all schools preparing students for the matric board exams used the same provincial government textbooks. In-house subject specialists at each provincial textbook board, a government body, wrote the textbooks or they commissioned university teachers or professors to write the books. Once the federal curriculum wing approved these books, the provincial textbook boards published and distributed them.

In the past ten years, two new policies have changed who is responsible for defining the curriculum and writing the textbooks. The 2007 National Textbooks and Learning Materials Policy mandated that the textbook boards were no longer to write textbooks. Instead, the provincial governments would select the winning textbooks from submissions by private publishers; the idea was that competition would yield better textbooks.

Then the eighteenth amendment to Pakistan's constitution, passed in 2010, handed over curriculum responsibility to the provinces (this was part of system-wide decentralization of authority to the provinces; the federal ministry of education was abolished altogether). As a result, new curriculum authorities were established in each province, which can write their own curricula. The authorities are also responsible for the selection of textbooks through a competition among private publishers. In practice, the provinces are still, by and large, following federal curriculum guidelines and have yet to write their own comprehensive curriculum documents, though they certainly have taken leeway in their adaptations or interpretations of the latest federally developed curriculum. The textbook boards are now mere distribution authorities, although in cases where the competition among publishers doesn't yield usable textbooks, they may still write them.

The disadvantage of the new system is that private publishers need not have any subject knowledge and may be in the business only for the profits, as the government contract is lucrative.[13] The curriculum authority has substantial leeway in awarding the contract, raising the potential for corruption. Both factors could undermine the quality of the textbooks and were expressed to me as concerns by senior members of the Punjab Textbook Board in 2013. Indeed, I have observed that the books produced by private publishers are poorly written relative to those produced by the textbook boards.

THE IMPORTANCE OF THE TEXTBOOKS

The government textbooks are all generally low quality, thin volumes. In the Pakistan Studies textbooks, subjective statements are presented as facts without any references or opposing points of view. But they reign supreme in classrooms, and the board exams are directly, and exclusively, based on these textbooks. The exams reward rote memorization of the textbook material.

Over the course of my fieldwork across government, private, and nonprofit high schools in Punjab, I attended Pakistan Studies classes as an observer. In a typical classroom, the teachers taught a couple of pages of the textbook per lecture, repeating the sentences in the book with little explanation and no additional learning materials beyond the textbook. At times, the teacher asked a favorite student to read aloud a paragraph from the textbook. As the teacher or the student read aloud, the other students swayed slightly back and forth as if in a trance; they were rote learning the content.

The teachers go through the material in the textbooks two to three times over the course of the academic year, and repeatedly test the students. Neither the teachers nor the students question the logic underlying the textbook material in class, nor do they engage in any debate on the information in the books. Classes do not veer from the topic at hand, although in some cases I saw that teachers referred to examples from current news or historical examples as further illustrations of the topic. Things are stricter in government schools, and slightly more relaxed in private schools, where you might see a question or two from students or even a class discussion—which never happened in the government schools I visited (partially because of their large class sizes).

Thus there is no critical thinking, or plain thinking, to speak of in these classrooms. This is not exclusive to Pakistan Studies classes. This is the typical teaching style across courses in the government curriculum, and it is partly because these teachers are required to teach to the matric exam. This style of learning also stems from a hierarchical structure of society, which means information is consumed without question from those in positions of authority—in this case, teachers. This, we will see, plays a role in how these students think.

A CONSPIRACY-TINGED VIEW OF THE WORLD

Having placed these textbooks in the context of the Pakistani educational system, let's return to them. The insecure view of the world reflected in the textbooks begins with the story of Pakistan's inception and with the issue of the division of assets between the new countries and the Radcliffe border award that divided India and Pakistan on the map in 1947: "a conspiracy was planned by the Congress [party] in collaboration with Lord Mountbatten to complete the process of partition in such a manner as a truncated, imbalanced and weak Pakistan was made that would be compelled to be part of India soon."[14] The paranoia of the Indian threat is palpable.

The books are wary of the West and of America. The West is considered to be "two-face[d]," to work against Pakistan's interests, and to have betrayed Pakistan historically.[15] This idea figures prominently in the discussion on East Pakistan's secession in 1971, which gets a significant bit of attention in the Pakistan Studies books. The books state the independence of Bangladesh to be the work of a "secret agreement of big powers."[16] The United States, though mentioned only a few times in the textbooks, is singled out in this regard: "the process of separation of East Pakistan was secretly supported by America."[17] The United States is also described as having blocked and punished Pakistan's nuclear program and nuclear tests, while turning a blind eye toward India's program.

The textbook narrative on 1971 also emphasizes the "negative role of Hindu teachers" in East Pakistan and Indian interference: "India had a constant wish to weaken the integrity of Pakistan for one reason or another."[18] The textbooks do mention the political problems between East and West Pakistan that were the ultimate cause of the secession, but place more importance on foreign conspiracies and the Hindu role in East Pakistan.

The books clearly identify with "Muslim causes" across the globe, with the Palestinians versus the Israelis. (The most negative mention I came across was the following: "The wicked Jews put a portion of Masjid-e-Aqsa on fire to demolish it."[19] This phrase was removed after the 2006 curriculum reform, which is discussed later.) And the books state Pakistan's foreign policy and loyalties plainly: "The main objective of Pakistan's foreign policy is to protect the ideological borders of Pakistan . . . it can protect its ideology only by establishing better relations with the Islamic countries . . . the main reason for close contacts with the western countries is economic aid which made Pakistan closer to America and the western world."[20] And while one can argue with this policy, the statement itself is a pretty fair description of reality.

The textbooks, even the most recent ones, do not have an open discussion on terrorism or extremism in Pakistan. Terrorism is mentioned twice in the latest textbooks in the chapter on world affairs. First is the statement, "Pakistan supported America in Afghan war but as a consequence Pakistan itself is facing terrorism."[21] Second: "Pakistan is playing a very effective role against terrorism and extremism in the world."[22] There is not enough material there to affect readers' views on terrorism directly. The effect of the textbooks on student views on terrorism, as I will argue, is more indirect.

LITTLE PLACE FOR MINORITIES OR ETHNICITIES

Given the focus on Islam, Pakistan's religious minorities are generally relegated to an afterthought in the Pakistan Studies books—protections for them and their rights are usually stated at the end of the books, but they are, by and large, ignored otherwise. Jinnah's August 11, 1947, speech to the Constituent Assembly is mentioned in some of the textbooks at the end, in showcasing equal rights for minorities—but in many instances, the separation between religion and the state that Jinnah also outlined in that speech is (no doubt purposefully) left out.

Religious minorities are not the only ones left out of these books—ethnic differences are glossed over as well. Pakistan Studies textbooks mention only the most superficial cultural differences between the country's four provinces and omit any mention of their unique ethnic histories. This follows from the threat the Pakistani state feels from the country's different ethnicities. The provinces and their differences get just six sentences in the latest Pakistan Studies book from Punjab, striking in their banality:

All four provinces of Pakistan have their provincial cultures. There are differences in civilization to some extent, present in their customs and traditions and lifestyles. In spite of regional and lingual differences, with the passage of time, regional cultural similarities are thriving. Despite living in different regions people have the feeling of being close to each other and have a sense of being linked to each other. This gives birth to integration and cohesion. National identity is strengthened which is quite encouraging.[23]

Note the forced, contrived leap from difference to cohesion.

The frictions between the provinces and the center are glossed over entirely. Baluchistan has engaged in five insurgencies against the Pakistani state, the fifth one ongoing, but these go unmentioned. To be fair, it might be unrealistic to expect more, yet this is noteworthy precisely because it is consistent with a state that ignores its ethnicities.

Ethnic heroes, too, go unmentioned. The Pashtun leader Abdul Ghaffar Khan, also known as Bacha Khan, is considered a hero for opposing British colonial rule through nonviolence. But he resisted the original Pakistan movement before swearing allegiance to the new state. After 1947, he also resisted Pakistan's efforts at centralization; he wanted more autonomy for his province, then the North West Frontier Province (NWFP); he quickly became an anti-hero for the new Pakistani state. There is no mention of him in the textbooks. On the other hand, some Pakistan Studies textbooks revere the Jamaat's leader Maududi. Maududi had also resisted the original Pakistan movement, like Bacha Khan, yet the textbooks describe Maududi as one of the intellectual founders of that movement. The Jamaat influence is, thus, palpable in the pages of Pakistan's textbooks, implemented through JI rankers who populated the education bureaucracy during Zia's time.[24]

There is no room in the books for non-Muslim heroes, including those who resisted British rule and played a key role in the fight for independence. Eras of Hindu and Buddhist rule, too, are ignored. In high school textbooks, the coverage of history begins in the twentieth century, with the Pakistan movement. Middle school history textbooks typically begin with Muhammad bin Qasim, the first Muslim to arrive in the subcontinent.[25] (They, in fact, claim that he was the first Pakistani citizen—in keeping with a literal read of the two-nation theory that argues that Pakistan was "created" with the arrival of Muslims in the subcontinent.) Those middle school books cover the Muslim empires of the subcontinent but skip the Hindu empires.

It is clear that the Pakistani state uses its history textbooks to get its view of the world across directly and explicitly—and which state does not? Pakistan does so through the rest of its curriculum, as well. Religion is mentioned in the English and Urdu textbooks; even science textbooks are not immune. According to Pervez Hoodbhoy, science textbooks are required to begin by stating that Allah created the earth.[26] Students are not required to study world history to place Pakistan's history in any sort of context. In 2013, I asked a senior official at the federal curriculum wing (whose prerogative is now limited to the capital Islamabad and universities) about the possibility of making world history a core subject. His response: "Why would our students need to study world history when they live in Pakistan?"

I do not analyze core Islamic studies textbooks in detail here; they broadly deliver a literal interpretation of the religion. Shiraz Thobani characterizes the Islamic studies curriculum as "literalistic in its reading of the Quran . . . ahistorical . . . homogenizing . . . [and] prescriptive."[27] The bigger problem, in my view, is that many of the Islamiat teachers in government schools are unqualified to teach because they only have a madrassa degree. The Pakistani government has granted these degrees, the highest level of madrassa certification, equivalence to a regular university degree. (Madrassas are discussed further in the next chapter.) Madrassa-educated Islamiat teachers bring their biases from madrassas into the government schools where they teach: a fundamentalist reading of religion at the least, and extremism at the worst. Rote learning of the textbooks is likely advantageous to the students in this respect, because these biased teachers can influence students less with their personal views in the classroom.

A REFORM

In response to mounting criticism of biases in the curriculum, General Pervez Musharraf, then president, set a curriculum reform process in motion in 2004 that culminated in the revised National Curriculum of 2006. The writing of new textbooks using the 2006 curriculum was staggered, and new Pakistan Studies books were only introduced years later, in the 2012–13 school year for Punjab, Khyber Pakhtunkhwa (KPK), and Baluchistan. My analysis of the textbooks previously discussed is based on both the pre- and post-reform Pakistan Studies textbooks, and indicate that the effect of the curriculum reform, ultimately, was marginal.

The aims of the reform outlined by the Ministry of Education were narrow to begin with—not taking on or altering the historical narrative but, instead, simply aiming to remove problems, including negative language—and the reform was further diluted in the conversion of the curriculum to the textbooks. Historical errors, distortions, and biases, pervasive in the old textbooks, persist in the new ones. The improvements are mainly those of language and consist of removing negative allusions and softening the tone. The word *evil* is removed from the textbooks. *Enemy* is used a lot less, as is *jihad*.

This is an improvement, no doubt. But it is worth noting that the word *jihad* was not mentioned at all in the 2006 curriculum documents; it was added intentionally in the conversion of the curriculum to the textbooks. In a telling incident narrated to me by an Oxford University Press (OUP) executive in Pakistan, the OUP submitted textbooks to the competition among publishers in Punjab but was asked by the review committee to reintroduce the word jihad to the submitted textbook, even though the curriculum documents do not mention jihad. The review committee also asked OUP to portray Jinnah as very religious. The textbook was still not selected as the official textbook. Thus the official textbook review committees (part of the new provincial curriculum authorities) are holding back the reform, even relative to its limited outline.

One of the revised textbooks discusses Musharraf's policy of "enlightenment." The book states: "Musharraf changed the curriculum and tried to make it enlightened . . . but the religious people of Pakistan made it a failure."[28] It is ironic and telling that the textbook itself acknowledges the failed curriculum reform, given that it ostensibly follows the new 2006 curriculum. The pushback is clear.

This pushback, evidenced from these examples, occurred at each step of the way. It extended from those outlining the reform vision to those writing up the new curriculum documents, from the authors of the new textbooks to the textbook review committees, teachers, and examiners. It seems many of these people simply do not buy into the idea of reform, as they are products of the old education system themselves.

Another reason the reform essentially failed, in my view, is related to what development economist Lant Pritchett describes as the issue of "isomorphic mimicry." That is, weak, developing states "pretend to do the reforms that *look* like the kind of reforms that successful [countries] do, but without their core underlying functionalities."[29] Pakistan's education system went through the motions of a curriculum reform, as it were, without actually changing much.

The 2006 curriculum reform included teaching methods goals to reduce the emphasis on rote memorization in schools. These were implemented, for example, by introducing multiple-choice questions in textbooks and in exams, but the new questions still test memory. As an example, they ask about dates that are so close to each other that the students have no choice but to memorize them. And essay questions still reward rote learning; thus the teachers still fully engage in it. The teaching methods goal of the reform—with the intent to introduce analytical thinking—has been diluted almost entirely.

The prospects for future curriculum reform are weak. Islamists are a powerful counterforce and are quick to block and loudly denounce any news of the slightest reform as anti-Islam and pro-West. In 2015, the current emir of the Jamaat, Siraj-ul-Haq, was quoted as saying to students that "western NGOs were depriving our youth of their faith and ideology in the name of education and the government had given them a free hand to achieve their evil designs. There could not be a greater misfortune than handing over our new generation to the enemy."[30] In Khyber Pakhtunkhwa, the Jamaat—a coalition partner of the ruling Pakistan Tehreek-e-Insaf party—is reversing parts of the curriculum reform as implemented by the previous regime of the liberal Awami National Party. KPK has removed mentions of important non-Muslim figures of the subcontinent, as well as an essay on Helen Keller, and pictures of girls without their heads covered. It has added Quranic verses to science textbooks and has reintroduced mentions of jihad.

STUDENT ATTITUDES

We know what Pakistani high school students learn about history and about the world in school. How do they think about the rest of the world and their own country? In 2013 and 2014, my research assistants and I visited twenty-three high schools in Punjab and, after attending classes, talked with students in focus group settings, and with teachers one-on-one. Schools were randomly selected from the full set of schools registered with the Lahore board of secondary education. These included girls' as well as boys' schools, urban and rural schools, government schools, private schools, and nonprofit schools in Lahore and Sheikhupura. The private schools varied from low-cost to elite (the elite private school and nonprofit school were selected nonrandomly for a deliberate comparison). All of these schools followed the government curriculum; the elite school also conducted O-level classes.

There are a few things to note about Lahore and Sheikhupura and the representativeness of the interviews in Punjab relative to the rest of the country. The study focused on these two districts in northeastern Punjab, including the poorest and most rural parts of these districts, mainly because of security concerns in conducting research elsewhere. The population of the Lahore metropolitan area was estimated at 9.2 million as of July 2014, and the Sheikhupura metropolitan area at 3 million as of 2013.[31] Both districts are more urban, prosperous, and better connected on various dimensions than other parts of the country (these factors can affect student attitudes, but it is unclear in which direction *a priori*). Additionally, these two districts had not been the target of major, sustained terrorist attacks in the time period immediately prior to the interviews (although there certainly has been terrorist violence in Lahore, especially in 2008–09, and more recently, a large-scale attack at the Wahgah border in November 2014, at a Lahore park on Easter Sunday in 2016, and in front of the Punjab Assembly in February 2017); my interviewees may, thus, have a higher tolerance for terrorist groups than students in other parts of the country that have suffered violence more directly.

Punjab is Pakistan's most populous and prosperous province, and the seat of Pakistan's military, bureaucratic, and political establishment. It is generally considered more conservative and more representative of the "mainstream" views of Pakistani society (partly because of the sheer size of its population and through its dominance of the state apparatus).

We can contextualize attitudes in Punjab relative to the other provinces by analyzing the Pew survey data. I found that respondents from Punjab are the most favorable, and the least unfavorable, toward all four terror groups across provinces. Respondents from Sindh and Khyber Pakhtunkhwa have the least favorable views toward these groups. As an example, favorability for the Tehrik-e-Taliban Pakistan (TTP) is 23 percent for Punjabi respondents, and only 5 percent for respondents from Sindh. Respondents from KPK are also the most unfavorable toward each of the terror groups.

Also, according to the survey data, respondents in Punjab are the most unfavorable toward India across provinces, and are very unfavorable toward the United States. KPK is the most anti-American province, while Sindh has the highest favorability toward India across provinces. Baluchistan has high nonresponse rates across provinces for all the questions about terror groups and about India and the United States.

Baluchistan has been engulfed in a separatist insurgency for decades, and fierce state repression in response; thus Baluchis' nervousness is understandable. KPK has borne the brunt of the TTP's terror. The province's disdain for all terrorist groups—and not just the one that targets it—is clear and is accompanied by anti-Americanism (driven at least partly by its proximity to Afghanistan). Sindh has a rich Sufi tradition. It is liberal and nonconformist, and dominated by Karachi, a cosmopolitan metropolis that has also seen a great deal of violence, including by the Taliban. From this data, Punjab is the clear "extreme" across the provinces in terms of favorability for terror groups and is the most negative toward other countries. It is worth keeping this in mind as we discuss students' attitudes in the schools I visited in Punjab.

Discussions at the selected schools began with current events. Both the students and their teachers were asked about the major problems Pakistan was facing at the time; how they would rank terrorism as one of those problems; the causes of terrorism in their view; the groups involved in terrorism; and how terrorism could be fixed. They were also asked about the United States, and about India, and minorities. Many of the discussions lasted well over an hour. The students were incredibly open and willing to share their views, and were all friendly, earnest young people, exceedingly generous with their time. I'm grateful to them for helping me understand what was on their minds.

Much of what they said reflects the views of the narrative mainstream represented in the first chapter in this book. What follows is a summary of these students' responses. On terrorism, responses could be classified into one of four sets. One set argued the causes of terrorism were economic; that terrorism stems from poverty, unemployment, lack of education, and inequality—following a conventional wisdom on the topic that we will come back to. In the words of a female student from the nonprofit school in Lahore: "People have taken a wrong meaning of Islam. They think that Islam says this is how to do jihad. But that is not right. They come toward this because of poverty—if they had a job they wouldn't." I heard this from female teachers and students more than from anyone else. Another set of responses blamed Pakistan's own government—politicians, the police, and their corruption—for causing terrorism, but did not explain or elaborate on this view.

The third explanation, the dominant one among these students, blamed "foreign influences"—the United States and India—for the attacks, whether as a conspiracy theory or arguing that terrorism is a response to U.S. actions such as drone strikes. This type of response was discussed in detail in chapter 1. The final explanation argued that the country is currently on the wrong, un-Islamic path, and that terrorists "merely" want to implement Islam in Pakistan.

Terrorism is barely mentioned in the textbooks, so while we can say these views are not directly derived from the books, it is easy to see the roots of the conspiracy-style argument for terrorism, and blaming India and the West for it, in the textbooks. The distrust of the West and the paranoia of India that are significant themes in the books are consistent with the students blaming India and the United States for terrorism, as is the idea that "Muslims can't kill other Muslims," given how the textbooks always portray Muslims as good and as victims. You can also see the roots of the responses that terrorists want an Islamic system in Pakistan in the textbooks' focus on Islam, in the repetition of the idea that Pakistan was created for Islam, and in the books' references to jihad.

The United States looms large in the consciousness of these high school students, either as conspiring against Pakistan or forcing it into the U.S.-Afghan war (on the U.S. side) post-2001. Respondents brought it up themselves early on in the discussions when we talked about the causes of terrorism in Pakistan. Later in the interviews, when asked about America directly, they talked about the different treatments of Raymond Davis and Aafia Siddiqui and the raid that killed Osama bin Laden. The themes of American bullying, betrayal, and hypocrisy kept recurring. In the interviews conducted in 2013, when drone strikes in Pakistan were at their peak, the students mentioned these strikes repeatedly.

We can trace these views to the sparing mentions of the United States in the Pakistan Studies textbooks. They offer a skeleton of a narrative of the United States—a power that favors India relative to Pakistan (by trying to thwart Pakistan's nuclear ambitions) and that betrayed Pakistan in 1971. This sets the stage for respondents' attitudes toward the United States, that are then filled in by narratives in the media, the narratives of politicians, and how society discusses America. Students seamlessly absorb the references to Osama bin Laden (OBL) and Raymond Davis and Aafia Siddiqui as they are mentioned in the media. The perception of OBL's killing as a blow to Pakistan's national sovereignty, for example, is a direct product of the Pakistan military's press strategy in the wake of that event. In Pakistan, the initial attention after the OBL raid was focused on the Pakistani military's incompetence or complicity in hiding bin Laden.[32] Within a couple of days, Pakistan's army chief forcefully shifted the discussion to a violation of Pakistan's sovereignty.[33]

Conspiracy theories about the United States running every-thing in Pakistan are especially prevalent in the Urdu-language media and on social media,[34] and matric students are avid con-sumers of that media. In their focus groups, they sometimes refer-enced videos or photographs they had seen online: "There was a place they showed in America, where there were religious Islamic men [*maulvis*], with long beards, who were being taught the Qur-an, but they were all kafirs [nonbelievers]—they were being sent in the midst of Muslims to derail/sidetrack Muslims"—in the words of a male student in a private school. The conspiracy-mongering textbooks encourage them to buy in to such stories.

Two students interviewed in focus groups, a girl and a boy from separate public schools, stood out with more radical views than the others. This does not imply, however, that they would become violent. They were both followers of Muhammad Ilyas Attar Qa-dri's fundamentalist group Dawat-e-Islami, the same group that Mumtaz Qadri, Taseer's assassin, belonged to (he had adopted Attar Qadri's last name as his own). The male student was also a madrassa student, a Hafiz-e-Quran (a term for those who memo-rize the Quran), and a deputy imam (the deputy leader) at a mosque. In his view, terrorism was justified in terms of religion: "The day our leaders start following the examples of Khulfa-e-Rashideen [the Prophet's four companions and successors] and when there will be Nizam-e-Mustafa [the law of Muhammad] the terrorists themselves will give up. They are Muslims too and that is their only concern." For him, the religious cause was conflated with anti-Americanism: "People say Taliban are not willing to talk but actually the Taliban are willing to do this. But first we need to stop drone attacks. Actually we should launch operation against U.S. first, then against any other." In his view, Muslims had a duty to fight all enemies of Islam: "We need to follow the examples of Khulfa-e-Rashideen and fight against the enemies of Islam, 'dushman-e-Islam.'"

The girl with the more radicalized views was influenced by a pamphlet published by Dawat-e-Islami that she read in her home. Her family seemed to be followers of the group, as well.

Both, in their separate contexts, were able to influence their peers. They were loud and confident, spoke up frequently and clearly during our focus groups, and when they spoke, their fellow students would listen to them. The two often invoked religion with authority, which would make it difficult for the other students to counter them if they wanted to, as they could be accused either of not being religious or of being ignorant about religion—both problematic and dangerous in the context of Pakistan's blasphemy laws.

More fundamentally, the mainstream Pakistani education system does not enable or educate students so that they can counter such views—hence the classmates of these two students were vulnerable to their radical interpretations. Indeed, the two students themselves were incapable of countering the extremist propaganda they were exposed to—the boy in the madrassa and the girl at home, via pamphlets and her family—and so bought into that propaganda.

On the history with India and the two-nation theory, the overall student views were remarkably consistent with the textbooks, and almost homogenous within their focus groups. Where the students' responses went beyond the textbooks was in their view of India and its Research and Analysis Wing (RAW) being sponsors of terrorism in Pakistan because of their desire to destroy Pakistan, though this too is entirely consistent with the textbooks' portrayal of India as out to harm Pakistan.

Responding to the question of how religious minorities were treated in Pakistan—students were prompted about Shiites, Ahmadis, and Christians—students quickly invoked incidents of mistreatment of Muslims in America and India while sometimes undermining attacks on religious minorities within Pakistan. They reiterated the theoretical view from the textbooks, stating that minorities have equal rights in Pakistan. A few did acknowledge the attacks recently suffered by Christian churches and neighborhoods, but many seem removed from the reality of how these minorities are persecuted.

Students from urban, male, and private schools were more likely to offer more detailed descriptions of their views, but these views were no less extreme on average than those of students in rural, female, and government schools. The former groups seemed to be better exposed to various forms of media and had given greater thought to societal narratives. With the latter groups, there was more of a tendency to regurgitate something they had heard somewhere in passing.

It is striking that I did not observe large differences in attitudes across this sample of schools that employed the same, official curriculum, despite their varied teacher training, teaching methods, teacher-student interactions, and student socio-economic backgrounds. There is some variation among the students, to be sure, but it is marginal. Students do not contradict what is learned in schools, nor do they question it. They don't have the tools to do so. That they hold some of these views is not the fault of the students—it rests with what the state teaches them.

EDUCATION AND ATTITUDES

These were high school students. From the survey data, it is worth placing their attitudes in context relative to those of individuals with different education levels. This is best done with cross-tabulating views from the Pew survey data considered in chapter 1 with education levels. (The education levels of Pew respondents are found in appendix B, table B-2. I also confirm the results with regressions, which account for education, age, income, province, gender, and urbanity; unless otherwise noted, the regression results reveal the same patterns as the cross-tabulations.)

FIGURE 4-1. **Views toward Violence in the Name
of Islam by Education Level**

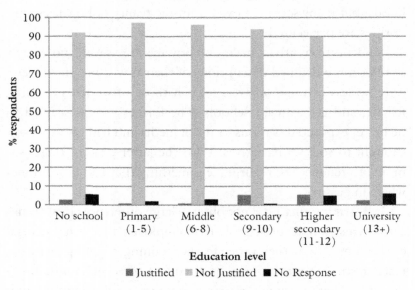

Source: Author's graph, using Pew Research Center's Global Attitudes Spring 2013 survey data for Pakistan
(www.pewglobal.org/datasets/2013/).
Interview Question: Some people think that suicide bombing and other forms of violence against civilian targets
are justified in order to defend Islam from its enemies. Other people believe that, no matter what the reason, this
kind of violence is never justified. Do you personally feel that this kind of violence is often justified to defend
Islam, sometimes justified, rarely justified, or never justified?

First, views on violence against civilians in the name of Islam do
not vary significantly with education (see figure 4-1). Ninety percent
or more of respondents believe such violence is not justified; this is
true across all education levels. The percentage of those who say
such violence is justified is tiny, 5 percent at its highest, notably at
the secondary and higher secondary levels—but this in itself is not
conclusive evidence of "worse" views at that level of education.

Second, let's look at views of terrorist groups according to
education. Figure 4-2 shows views of the TTP in 2013 across
education levels as an illustrative example. Across all four terror
groups—TTP, Lashkar-e-Taiba (LeT), al Qaeda (AQ), and the Afghan Taliban (AT)—and across years of polling data, two patterns
hold: first, better-educated individuals are more unfavorable toward

FIGURE 4-2. **Views of the TTP by Education Level**

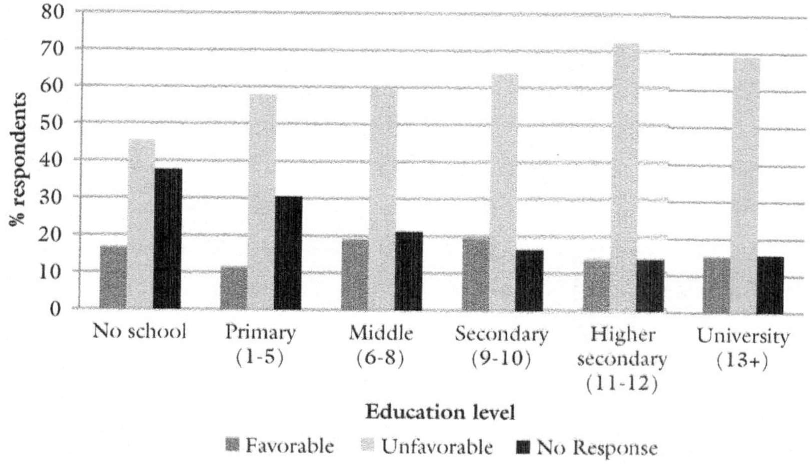

Source: Author's graph, using Pew Research Center's Global Attitudes Spring 2013 survey data for Pakistan (www.pewglobal.org/datasets/2013/).
Interview Question: Please tell me if you have a very favorable, somewhat favorable, somewhat unfavorable, or very unfavorable opinion of Tehrik-e-Taliban?

terror groups; second, education increases response rates to questions about these groups (presumably because it makes people more confident in their responses).

Favorability for terrorist groups is low across the board. Changes in favorability with varying education levels are slight and the direction of these changes is not consistent across terrorist groups and years. High school respondents are slightly *more* favorable toward the Afghan Taliban, the Pakistan Taliban, and LeT than are those students with less education. For the AT and TTP, favorability falls again for higher education levels. But for LeT, favorability keeps increasing beyond high school. It is worth defining the concept of *net unfavorability*, the percentage unfavorable minus the percentage favorable, at each education level. Net unfavorability rises unambiguously with education for all terror groups, as does the certainty of responses—so on net, education "improves" views.

It is notable that favorability itself doesn't fall with education and that it increases across terror groups around the secondary school level. Why does this happen? Partly because of lower nonresponse rates for these schooling levels—that is, their higher confidence in expressing their views—but there has to be an important answer in high school curricula, too, which, in their ideological nature and rote style, may worsen views for some students. For high school students, their education gives them a framework to accept a radical outlook and does not give them the critical skills to counter it. University education helps reduce favorability again—though not below what it is for those who are illiterate.

That favorability for LeT rises across education levels indicates that educated Pakistanis think somewhat differently about LeT than about other terror groups. There are likely a number of reasons for this: LeT's provision of charity, its Kashmiri cause, and its highly educated leader, Hafiz Saeed. But it's worth noting that net unfavorability rises consistently with education for the LeT, as well.

These empirical results add to the evidence on the relationship between education and attitudes. The conventional wisdom and the early thinking on radicalization posited the radicalized as poor, uneducated, unemployed young men, in Pakistan as well as in other contexts. The notion held that there was a linear, positive relationship between education and attitudes, and income and attitudes. But as Alan Krueger has documented extensively and exhaustively, a host of empirical studies in various country contexts showed no consistent relationship between education and views on terror groups.[35] The conventional wisdom stood debunked, yet it still persists. As an example, Punjab's Chief Minister Shahbaz Sharif recently stated that more education "will comprehensively defeat terrorism and militancy."[36] Pakistan's ex-president Musharraf stated it simply in a speech at Stanford University in 2009: "Poverty, illiteracy cause terrorism."[37] That notion persists in the United States as well, with the provision of economic and development assistance to Pakistan (in particular under the Enhanced Partnership with Pakistan Act of 2009, informally called the Kerry-Lugar-Berman Act) that also aims to counter extremism.

In contrast to Krueger's work, the bulk of my analysis shows an overall improvement in views on terrorist groups with education in Pakistan, supporting the conventional wisdom. But looking at favorability alone lends support to those who debunk the conventional wisdom (and, indeed, some of this literature does look at favorability alone, which is why it may be missing the bigger picture). The question of why education does not reduce favorability is in itself important. The narratives of high school students lend further support to the fact that education does not work quite as we would like it to.

At this juncture, a quick note is in order on how income, gender, and age impact views on terrorist groups. My regression analysis reveals that respondents with higher incomes have more certain and more unfavorable views toward terrorist groups—the latter is true for all groups other than for Lashkar-e-Taiba. That is partially in line with the conventional wisdom that higher incomes improve attitudes. But views toward LeT are different—that is, higher earners are no more likely to have unfavorable views toward LeT than those earning less; the reason could be the group's rhetoric, its Indian target, or its charity. Women have less certain and less unfavorable views toward terrorist groups than men—likely because of relative segregation for men and women in Pakistan and women's lower exposure to the political and security narrative. Older Pakistanis tend to have both less favorable and more unfavorable views toward terror groups—that is, younger Pakistanis have more "extreme" views, worrisome given the country's demographics. The country faces a youth bulge, with fifteen to twenty-nine year olds accounting for 46 percent of its total population.[38] Thus should nothing else change, because of demographics alone attitudes will worsen over time as those in the older generations pass away.

Returning to schooling, how do views of India and the United States change with education? Views of India worsen for the initial years of education, and begin improving in secondary school.

FIGURE 4-3. **Views of India by Education Level**

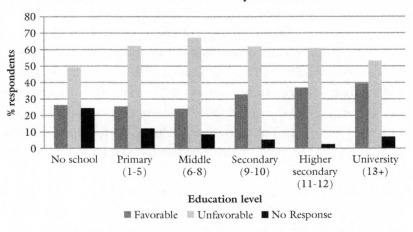

Source: Author's graph, using Pew Research Center's Global Attitudes Spring 2013 survey data for Pakistan (www.pewglobal.org/datasets/2013/)
Interview Question: Please tell me if you have a very favorable, somewhat favorable, somewhat unfavorable, or very unfavorable opinion of India?

Figure 4-3 shows that favorability toward India rises with education, and nonresponse falls, but unfavorability rises until middle school and declines beyond it. Thus in the initial years of education net unfavorability (unfavorability minus favorability) toward India rises—unsurprising given the content of school textbooks, and falls later; it is at its lowest at the university level. Regressions reveal a somewhat different story; after accounting for province, gender, age, and income, the effects of education on favorability seen in the graph do not appear to hold in the regression, but there is higher unfavorability at each education level when compared to unfavorability for no schooling; only at the university level is unfavorability not higher relative to no schooling. This offers a damning indictment of the textbooks.

We see a similar pattern for how views of America vary with education (figure 4-4). Education improves favorability toward the United States and lowers nonresponse; unfavorability rises at first with education and then declines, but it peaks at the higher secondary level, later than for India. Net unfavorability toward

FIGURE 4-4. **Views of the United States by Education Level**

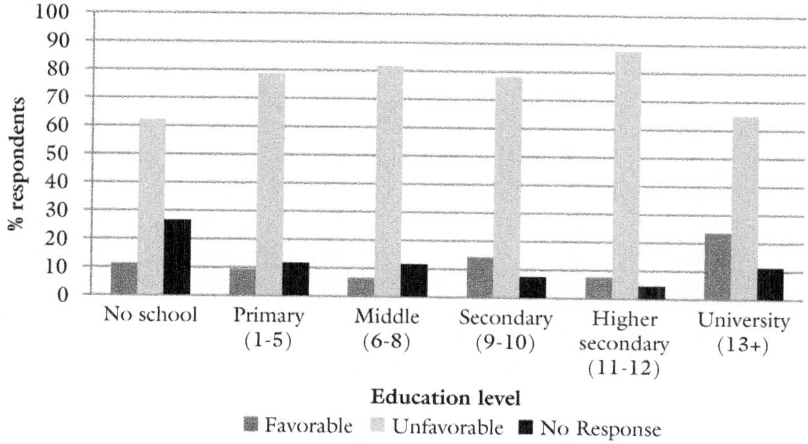

Education level
■ Favorable   ▨ Unfavorable   ■ No Response

Source: Author's graph, using Pew Research Center's Global Attitudes Spring 2013 survey data for Pakistan (www.pewglobal.org/datasets/2013/)
Interview Question: Please tell me if you have a very favorable, somewhat favorable, somewhat unfavorable, or very unfavorable opinion of the United States?

America is highest at the higher secondary level—much higher than for those with no schooling. University education helps soften views, reducing net unfavorability significantly (by both reducing unfavorability and increasing favorability)—this is discussed in the next section. The regressions show that favorability toward the United States is higher for those at the university level than for those with no education. Unfavorability is also higher for those at each education level relative to those with no education, except at the university level.

What about views of apostasy? Figure 4-5 shows how attitudes on the death penalty for those leaving Islam vary with education; the answer is not much. Education slightly increases favorability toward this punishment; nonresponse declines with more education. This speaks to how deeply religious sentiment—and belief in harsh punishment for denouncing religion—is ingrained in the entire population; and that education not only does not reduce it, it appears to cement it (confirmed by the regression). Pakistan's blasphemy laws play a role here.

FIGURE 4-5.   **Views on the Death Penalty for Those
Leaving Islam by Education Level**

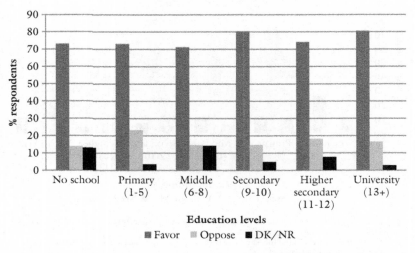

Source: Author's graph, using the Pew Forum on Religion and Public Life's The World's Muslims November 2011 Survey data for Pakistan (www.pewforum.org/2013/04/30/the-worlds-muslims-religion-politics
-society-overview/)
Interview Question (asked of Muslims only): Do you favor or oppose the following: the death penalty for those
who leave the Muslim religion?

To sum up, some views change little with education—such as attitudes on violence against civilians in the name of Islam, roundly condemned; or the death penalty for leaving Islam, broadly agreed on across education levels. A lack of education does not make people prone to approving violence, and education doesn't make them give up the regressive interpretations of Islam propagated by the state through its laws. But education does move views on other countries and terrorism, and education beyond high school in particular seems to make people more open and more anti-extremist. A few years of education actually worsen views on India and the United States. Given the discussion on high school textbooks, this is far from a surprise, but attending university seems to set this right to a large extent. Education, on net, improves views on terrorist groups, although for the initial years of education this is also accompanied by rising favorability.

Let us take a deeper look at universities. Why do attitudes improve with university education in a way they do not after high school?

UNIVERSITIES

In May 2015, I (and a research assistant) visited the history departments of two prestigious, established government universities in Lahore, and held group discussions with their Master's students. We met day scholars and boarding students from all over the country. All the students we met had gone through the government school system, had matric and intermediate (higher secondary) degrees, had taken government board exams, and had studied the same Pakistan Studies textbooks described earlier. These university students serve as a good representation of where the high school students we met earlier would be a few years later. They would be the best of those students since they made it to good universities. Both focus groups were fascinating.

At the more elite university, our discussion was refreshingly open and lasted three hours. It was also strikingly left wing. The students, many of them from Baluchistan or KPK, talked at length about their deep distrust of the Pakistani army and state. They discussed the question of a secular versus Islamic Pakistan and refuted the notion that Pakistan was created for Islam. They discussed the importance of having an open conversation on religion. They seemed to question everything. They disagreed with each other, too. Not everyone was as skeptical of the state and the army; there was one notable pro-army voice in the group, a local Punjabi student. Students from Baluchistan and KPK and the tribal areas were the most alienated from the state; their views were farthest from the mainstream. This follows from their provincial backgrounds.

The students talked about how their Pakistan Studies textbooks in high school had tried to indoctrinate them ideologically, without teaching them the correct version of historical events, and said that they were only learning "true history" at university. They brought in examples from around the world, discussed American history, and quoted Chomsky. They referenced what they read in their courses. They seemed to read widely, especially newspapers.

Much of our discussion progressed without prompting on my part. Midway through our conversation, their teacher joined us. At first I was skeptical and thought he would constrain their responses (in none of my other group interviews with students had I allowed the teacher to sit in), but it soon became apparent that the teacher was a major influence on their thinking and was a sounding board for their ideas.

He himself explained his views of the Pakistan ideology: "Pakistan was not created for Islam but to secure the economic rights of Muslims. The real purpose was the welfare of Muslim population, as political development began. There was no focus on Shariat" pre-partition. His view was that the two-nation theory was constructed to fit the political movement and to give it momentum.

The students discussed Jinnah's contradictory statements on religion in Pakistan and the inherent tension in the creation of Pakistan given the fact that more Muslims stayed behind, or were left behind (relative to the numbers who migrated), in India. They considered minorities to be treated badly in Pakistan. They were clearly influenced by their questioning teacher and by learning history from around the world. They also recognized that their dissenting views could land them in danger. In the words of one student, "in Pakistan, if somebody doesn't follow the state narrative that person is a threat, a traitor."

Their views veered so much to the left, and they were so critical of the state, that all of Pakistan's troubles seemed to them as if driven by a state-run conspiracy. This is where they seemed least rational.

At the larger, more conservative of the two universities, the focus group was different but no less fascinating. There we saw that one of the students in particular gave voice to the same amalgam of conspiracy theories as we saw in high schools and in mainstream Pakistani society—that RAW, MOSSAD, the CIA are "behind" terrorism in Pakistan, that these agencies and their countries want to undermine the China Pakistan Economic Corridor. Education does not necessarily eliminate these views. As we know from chapter 2, educated politicians also propagate such views. The student just mentioned also invoked drone strikes, and he argued that terrorism occurred in retaliation to such strikes. Yet a second student in that focus group was on the other end of the spectrum, his views liberal and fact based. He placed the burden for terrorism on the Afghan jihad of the 1980s: "America needed jihadis to disintegrate Russia and we promoted jihad. We created a mindset and we successfully disintegrated Russia but that mindset remained there which thinks that change is only possible through jihad. . . . Those jihadis turned into terrorists." Others stood between these students on the spectrum.

What was notable was the internal consistency in the students' views for those on either end of the spectrum; we can "bucket" them as progressive or conservative. Their views of minorities, for instance, correlated with their views on terrorism. The liberal student I described above argued that minorities were persecuted in Pakistan as a result of the blasphemy law: "[Zia's] era was one of too much Islamization. We introduced many laws to make people more Muslim, such as the blasphemy law. Before this law there were one or two cases of blasphemy but after this law people started using it for their personal purposes." The other student (the one touting conspiracy theories), however, had more of a mainstream view on minorities; he argued that minorities were treated as equals in Pakistan, that terrorist attacks targeted Muslims in Pakistan as well, and that Muslims in the United States were not well treated.

All the students were able to explain the nuances of their views, in contrast to the high school students. In showing how RAW was "behind terrorism," one student told us: "If we see in Baluchistan the youth such as boys of twenty-five to twenty-seven years old, they are M.A. pass [they hold a Master's degree] but they don't have jobs. The insurgents give them 5,000 to 10,000 salary from RAW and ask them go and kill some F.C. [Frontier Corps, the paramilitary force in KPK and Baluchistan] guy and they do it for 5,000 to 10,000 rupees." He was arguing that these "outside funders" could exploit poverty and unemployment to recruit men toward terrorism.

I did not have to ask many questions here, either. We needed to work harder to direct the conversation in my high school interviews. Yet the increase in nuance, and in dissenting and open views relative to high school, are unmistakable. Other students talked about the problem with madrassas teaching extremism and with sectarianism. They read widely, both the Urdu and English press.

The students from these two universities, while they are likely a select group of the brightest graduates from government schools and colleges, do not belong to an elite, liberal segment of society (that group would not go to government schools to begin with; therefore the selection of bright, liberal students into universities cannot explain away the liberal views I observed. And neither can the provincial differences between the interviewees—recall that my most liberal interviewees were from Baluchistan and KPK). As I discussed, when I ran regressions using the survey data to look at the effect of education on attitudes, I found that even after controlling for provinces, university education improves views toward the United States and India, and reduces support for terror groups (especially relative to high school).

It looks like the history taught at the university level matters, as do better teachers. Students and teachers are less shackled by exams, which no longer reward pure memorization, allowing them to flex their thinking muscles and to have class-based discussions.

Things are different for those students who study pure sciences— such as engineering or medicine. Their view of history is unlikely to change much because they are only required to take Pakistan Studies and Islamic Studies (and language) as non-science courses.

Their Pakistan Studies texts propagate the same historical myths as do the high school textbooks, and their learning continues to be rote-based, as are their exams. So they do not develop the same critical thinking skills that humanities and social science university students develop. Perhaps this partly explains the popularity of the LeT at one of Pakistan's premier government engineering universities (University of Engineering and Technology, Lahore). Of course, that's also where Hafiz Saeed, LeT's founder, taught for many years.

This shows that the effects of the biased education from government curricula are reversible. But the reversal does not come only from more years of education; it comes through greater exposure to world history, an interactive classroom discussion, and a teaching style that asks questions as much as provides answers.

THE ALTERNATIVE

The gulf between the majority of Pakistani students represented above and the segment studying for the Cambridge-administered O-level board exams is so wide that it led the Pakistani academic Tariq Rahman to term the two "denizens of alien worlds." O-level students must also take Pakistan Studies as a core subject. I have analyzed those textbooks, and provide an overview of them here. As we will see, O-level students have better textbooks and more tolerant attitudes than the matric students.

The starkest difference with the matric textbooks is that the "Pakistan ideology" is nowhere to be found in the O-level Pakistan Studies books. The books are objective, not ideological, and Islam does not figure prominently in them. We know the matric textbooks center themselves on the religious ideology construct.

Second, the O-level history books tell the evolving political story of partition, in contrast to the linear narrative presented in the matric books. Both the matric and the Cambridge books cover the march to independence, with a similar narrative arc focusing on the same key points in history, but the treatment of the material in the Cambridge books is vastly different and superior. A major topic in the curriculum is "how important were attempts to find a solution to the problems facing the subcontinent in the years 1940 to 1947."[39] The Cambridge texts describe the evolution of the two-nation theory and include prominent Muslim thinker Sir Syed Ahmed Khan's initial pronouncements about Hindus and Muslims being one nation. They describe periods of Hindu-Muslim cooperation. They also mention Jinnah's initial opposition to partition before explaining how events changed his mind and led to "the parting of the ways" between Hindus and Muslims.[40]

The O-level textbooks also show the positive side of India and Hindus along with the negatives. Upon partition, when India withheld the cash it owed Pakistan, they state that "Gandhi was determined that the division of assets should be as fair as possible. He objected to what the Indian government was doing."[41] The books state that Gandhi began a hunger strike, and, as a result, the Indian government paid Pakistan the remaining 500 million rupees it was owed. This incident is not mentioned in the matric books, which fixate on Pakistan as a victim in the division of assets at partition.

The O-level books acknowledge the bloodshed on both sides during partition: "In the summer of 1947 emotions ran so high that ordinary, peace-loving Hindus, Sikhs and Muslims became caught up in acts of violence of which they would never have considered themselves capable."[42] It is hard to think of a better treatment of this difficult topic.

The books soundly discuss the topic of minorities in Pakistan. They quote Jinnah's critical statement: "You may belong to any religion, caste or creed—that has nothing to do with the business of the state." They also mention that Jinnah was called the "protector-general" of minorities. They discuss the *ulema* campaign against the Ahmadis starting in the early 1950s and mention the harmful effect of Zia's policies on minorities, and on Shias and Ahmadis in particular.

At times the O-level books directly refute the national narrative. The books state that Ayub Khan told the country that Pakistan had won the 1965 war but it had not.[43] The matric textbooks propagate Ayub's official line—that Pakistan won the war.

The events leading to 1971 are discussed honestly in the O-level textbooks, acknowledging West Pakistan's faults and its brutality in the secession. On the role the United States played in the 1971 war, the narrative in the O-level books is similar to the matric textbooks, which talk about the West deserting Pakistan in 1971, but with the important difference that it is not alluded to as a secret conspiracy.

On terrorism, there isn't much, because the books focus on pre-2000 material, but they have a clear-eyed discussion of Pakistan's support to Afghanistan's Taliban government in the 1990s. Benazir Bhutto is quoted on this in 2007, shortly before her death: "It was a critical, fatal mistake we made. If I had to do things over again, that's certainly not a decision that I would have taken."[44]

Finally, the stylistic differences are stark. Recall that the matric books present no sources, primary or secondary. There is no sense in them of historical research, of multiple representations of history. On the other hand, the O-level books have a great deal more nuance and objectivity than the matric books and clearly aim to create analytical, thinking citizens. The curriculum states that it aims to "develop [an] understanding of the nature and use of historical evidence," and the authors present an abundance of it in the textbooks: old speeches, the writings of prominent figures, historians' accounts. The books report how different sides represent the same historical event differently—for example, how 1857 was the "Indian mutiny" for British historians, but the "war of independence" for Indian historians. Questions are repeatedly posed to the reader—how, what, why—and these do not necessarily have one right or wrong answer. Students are asked to reconcile different accounts of the same event and to draw their own conclusions. The Cambridge exam rewards additional reading, questioning the material, and drawing deductions. Students read a variety of books in addition to textbooks—and therefore are exposed to a great deal of high-quality material.

There is certainly room for improvement. The first chapter in the O-level books is one on Islamic thinkers, and it stands out for its lack of historical context and nuance. Jihad is mentioned a number of times in that chapter, as is the importance of an Islamic way of life—although all by way of describing the Islamic thinkers' beliefs. The chapter also references Syed Ahmad Barelvi, who, you may remember, was described in the pre-2006 matric textbooks as conducting jihad against the "evil" Sikhs. The O-level books describe Barelvi's "struggle" but do not use the word "evil" in describing his foes: "Syed Ahmad founded the jihad movement, which called for armed struggle to overthrow non-Muslim oppression and restore Muslim power. He believed that once this was done, Islam could be rejuvenated and rescued from beliefs and customs contrary to Islamic beliefs which had crept into daily life."[45] It continues: "The jihad movement was a uniting force for Muslims. Many of Syed Ahmad's soldiers had been spiritual leaders or teachers. The fact that they were prepared to die for their cause was an inspiration to all Muslims."[46] This—equating jihad with an armed struggle, talking about conducting jihad to purify Islam—is worrisome. But the focus on religion is limited to this chapter.

These curricular differences matter. O-level students have better attitudes on a number of dimensions compared to matric students in Pakistan—on jihad and open war against India, and tolerance for minorities, at least according to a survey on student attitudes conducted by Tariq Rahman in elite and government schools in major cities in 2002 and 2003. The survey shows that O-level students are less likely than matric students to advocate for open war against India over Kashmir (26 percent versus 40 percent) and jihad against India over Kashmir (22 percent versus 33 percent). More O-level students support equal rights for minorities than matric students: 66 percent of O-level students versus 47 percent of matric students support equal rights for Ahmadis, 78 percent versus 47 percent support equal rights for Hindus, and 84 percent versus 66 percent for Christians.

Because more able students—better off and perhaps from more liberal families—select into elite schools to begin with, we cannot conclude that these differential attitudes reflect a causal effect of the different curricula on attitudes. But it is clear that the elite O-level curriculum sets the stage for its students to have reasoned thinking on these topics even when faced with propaganda in the media and elsewhere.

The two systems create two vastly different types of citizens. The Cambridge student is analytical, can think critically, understands how history evolves, understands what constitutes evidence, and how to assess multiple sources of evidence. He or she understands the political process leading to the creation of Pakistan and that there are two sides to every story. She can reason when faced with conspiracy theories. She has been challenged as part of understanding history. The matric student is, essentially, not prepared on any of these fronts and is particularly vulnerable to conspiracy theories. He or she does not know how to collect and evaluate evidence, having memorized the assigned textbooks. She has a one-sided view of the world in favor of Pakistan and Muslims. Her sense of nationhood and national identity is defined on the basis of religion alone. She is threatened by India and the West and considers Pakistan a victim. This student has a poor sense of her own country's history, having had to memorize a set of stereotypes.

Pakistan's media environment is segmented by language, and, by corollary, educational systems. The English-language news media leans to the left, with prestigious newspapers like *Dawn* taking the lead; while Urdu-language television and newspapers range from centrist to hyper-conservative, and frequently dabble in conspiracy theories and fake news. Students in the O-level system are generally consumers of English-language media; matric students tend to consume their news in Urdu. Thus the differences in their educational training are compounded by their media access: the matric graduate, already less able to resist propaganda, is also more likely to be exposed to it than the O-level graduate.

Consider, for instance, the matric students who heard Fazlullah's daily radio broadcasts in Swat in 2006 and 2007, declaring fatwas on girls' schools and jihad against the American "invaders"; would they be able to counter him?

Pakistan has seen recent examples of educated terrorists like Saad Aziz, a graduate of Karachi's prestigious Institute of Business Administration (IBA). Aziz killed the liberal activist Sabeen Mahmud in April 2015, and was implicated in an attack that killed forty-five members of the minority Ismaili community on a bus in Karachi that May.

Given that only a tiny percentage of the population, educated or otherwise, turns to violent extremism, prediction of radicalization based on terrorists' educational background or other sociodemographics is a nearly impossible and mostly pointless exercise. Something has to snap in order for someone even with extremist views to take the plunge toward violence: there is usually a deep sense of alienation, some desire for revenge, and a search for power in those who do. But how can someone educated at a prestigious university with an international-level curriculum become radicalized in the first place? We can say with some confidence that Saad Aziz's coursework at IBA did not radicalize him, but it also did not equip him to counter the militant propaganda that eventually did (he earned a BBA from IBA, a degree that does not tend to expose students to the humanities in Pakistan). He held a high school degree in the Cambridge system (an A-level degree) that should have trained him to think critically, but failed to. He appears to have been influenced by a co-worker he met during a summer internship at Unilever. A four-month-long "militancy training" in Miramshah, North Waziristan, after he had finished at IBA in 2011, seems to have cemented his radicalization.[47] But as we have seen in this chapter, people with Aziz's educational background generally tend to be less susceptible to extreme views and to radicalization than those with a public education; his outcome should be viewed as a relative exception.

We have seen that education, on net, improves views toward other countries and makes Pakistanis more unfavorable toward terrorist groups, but on other dimensions—such as the death penalty for apostasy—views do not change much with education. Favorability toward terrorist groups itself does not decline with education. Narratives improve with university education relative to high school education, and with O-level schooling relative to matric schooling. This suggests a role for reforming curricula to improve attitudes.

Curriculum reform in Pakistan is likely to be difficult—it has proven to be a political nonstarter, especially during democratic regimes; and even a well-intentioned, well-outlined reform is unlikely to fundamentally improve textbooks and teaching given the kind of systemic pushback seen in the mid-2000s. There is a deep skepticism of Western influence and opposition to "foreigners" writing Pakistani textbooks, limited not only to Islamists—it extends to nationalists as well. Recently, Bernadette Dean, a French academic who lived and worked in Pakistan, was forced to leave the country because she began receiving threats after it became known that she had coauthored some textbooks used by government schools.

Curriculum decisionmaking and, thus, the opposition to potential reform, are now decentralized to the provincial level. For Sindh, this is good news. Its Pakistan People's Party (PPP) government is likely more willing to undertake a reform, and Sindh is also less vulnerable than the other provinces to Islamist and nationalist influence to begin with (it may also need the reform less than the other provinces, since survey attitudes appear to be more tolerant there). For Punjab and KPK, the provincial decision-making means reform will be nearly impossible unless the provincial government proves capable of countering Islamist opposition. (Baluchistan may not have the capacity to undertake its own reform; it uses textbooks from Punjab.) Even if Sindh or another province decides to go forward with reform, the process of implementing it—the outlining of a new Pakistan Studies curriculum and writing of textbooks—will be difficult.

The analysis in this chapter yields a way forward. World history could be made a core subject in high schools, exposing students to multiple sides of history by design. To the extent that the O-level Pakistan Studies curriculum and textbooks already exist and are approved by the Pakistani government, it is arguably feasible to switch schools to these textbooks, translated into Urdu, relatively quickly (although the main O-level history textbook currently in use was written by Nigel Kelly, who is not Pakistani, there are good books written by Pakistanis as well, including one by Farooq Naseem Bajwa). These textbooks could be simplified in light of the poor academic training of matric students, but as long as their balanced, unbiased view and emphasis on analytical thinking is maintained, the benefits to students would accrue. Teachers would have to be trained to engage in classroom discussions, and the exams would have to be de-emphasized or at least made analytical to reward such discussions. The style of top-down learning will be difficult to upend entirely, because it is a societal phenomenon; yet engaging in discussion even on the margins, as seen in private schools and in the O-level system, benefits analytical thinking (recall that students I interviewed in private schools following the government curriculum could better explain their views).

This may be palatable to the provinces, although given the ruckus that Islamists and some in the Punjab provincial government recently created over the study of the reproductive system in sixth-grade textbooks in elite schools in Lahore, and over the subject of comparative religion taught in addition to Islamiat in these schools, there is reason to be skeptical about Punjab. KPK could be even worse, and as long as the Jamaat is a coalition partner, there is realistically little hope for change there.

FIVE

Islamists and Madrassas

Islamists do poorly in elections in Pakistan. Pakistan's two major Islamist parties, the Jamaat-e-Islami (JI) and the Jamiat Ulema-e-Islam Fazl (JUI-F), together currently hold only seventeen of the 342 seats in the National Assembly. Yet political Islamists exercise a powerful influence on the country disproportionate to their electoral strength, serving as coalition partners and providers of political capital to the major parties, whose mandate tends to be weak. The Jamaat maintains close ties with the establishment, is urban, hierarchical, and scholarly; the Jamiat is a grass-roots influencer through its rural mosques and madrassas.

The Jamaat-e-Islami is the more powerful of the two parties. It was founded pre-independence, in 1941, by Syed Abul A'la Maududi, an Islamic scholar and writer who focused on intellectual rigor. His Jamaat is a party characterized by "rigid hierarchy, urban focus, and hyper-intellectualism."[1] As a result, its appeal is limited to a literate, urban population. Its intellectual style aligns neatly

119

with students at universities, and its student wing, the Islami-Jamiat-e-Tulaba (IJT), is powerful, active, and strong-handed.

The JI was initially opposed to the idea of Pakistan, believing, instead, in a pan-Islamic ummah. But once it signed on to the Pakistan project, it focused its energies on the new country's constitution, wanting it to be an Islamic state. It helped ensure that the Objectives Resolution of 1949, the guide for Pakistan's future constitution, contained Islamic provisions. The JI pressured the Muslim League on an Islamic constitution in the early 1950s, though it was later pushed back because of its involvement in the 1953 anti-Ahmadi riots. It was Jamaat activism, too, that forced Ayub Khan to revert Pakistan to an Islamic Republic in 1963.

The Jamaat led the anti-Ahmadi movement in Pakistan. In 1953, Maududi published the virulently anti-Ahmadi pamphlet titled *Qadiani Masla* (*The Qadiani Problem*), which helped lead to the 1953 riots that killed hundreds of Ahmadis. In 1973, it was activists from the Jamaat's student wing who picked a fight with Ahmadis in Rabwah, instigating riots and an eventual 100-day campaign by the Jamaat and other Islamists to have Ahmadis declared non-Muslim. The campaign succeeded with Zulfikar Ali Bhutto's constitutional amendment in 1974.

Perhaps the Jamaat's greatest impact on Pakistan has been through its influence on the public education curriculum, detailed in the previous chapter. The JI espouses an ideal of Pakistan as an Islamic state, one free of foreign influence. Its current platform—from its manifesto for the May 2013 elections—is to end American "slavery to restore Pakistan's independence and sovereignty" and reestablish "a state similar to the one led by the Prophet Muhammad in Medina."[2]

The Jamaat is committed to nonviolence, but a number of prominent jihadists are former Jamaat rankers. Hafiz Saeed, the head of the anti-India Lashkar-e-Taiba (and its political arm, Jamaat-ud-Dawa), is a former member. Sufi Muhammad, the founder of the TNSM (Tehrik-e-Nifaz-e-Shariat-Mohammadi, a precursor of the Tehrik-e-Taliban Pakistan), was also a former JI leader. Sufi Muhammad quit the Jamaat in 1981 "citing irreparable ideological differences," essentially on the use of violence, and joined the Afghan jihad.[3] In 1989, he founded the TNSM in Dir to implement Sharia in the area. It is telling of the Jamaat's attitude toward extremists that it adopted a "judicious silence" toward the TNSM.[4]

The JUI-F, the second of Pakistan's prominent Islamist parties, was born when the Jamiat Ulema-e-Islam (JUI) split into two factions in the mid 1980s—the JUI-F, headed by Fazl-ur-Rehman, and the Jamiat Ulema-e-Islam Sami (JUI-S), headed by Sami-ul-Haq. The JUI-F, a current coalition partner of the ruling PML-N, does better electorally than the otherwise more powerful JI.

During the anti-Soviet jihad in the 1980s, the JUI was a major supplier of Afghan mujahideen. These fighters were trained in JUI madrassas, which mushroomed during General Muhammad Zia-ul-Haq's time. The party ran a large number of rural madrassas even before that, and derives much of its power from its rural madrassas and the mosques attached to them. The JUI and its splinter parties run more madrassas in Pakistan than any other religious organization.[5] Many local leaders of the JUI are madrassa-educated clerics.

While the JUI splinter parties do not engage in violence, they have close links with militants. Sami-ul-Haq is called the "father of the Taliban" because his Dar-ul-Uloom Haqqania madrassa at Akora Khattak is perhaps the most notorious madrassa for terrorist ties. It counts Mullah Omar as well as other Taliban leaders among its alumni. Fazl-ur-Rehman's faction has similar links. Wali-ur-Rehman, at one time the deputy chief of the Taliban, was a former member of the JUI-F.

In the 1990s, Fazl-ur-Rehman played an important role in Benazir Bhutto's government's support of the Afghan Taliban, helping it ascend to power in Afghanistan. At the time, his JUI-F was an ally of Bhutto's left, secular-leaning Pakistan People's Party government, and he was the chairman of the National Assembly's foreign affairs committee. His close ties with the Afghan Taliban have given him standing as the intermediary between Pakistan and the Afghan Taliban. Given the JUI's role in the Afghan jihad, it is no surprise these Islamists' sympathy for those who fought in it outlasted the exit of the Soviets.

Sami and Fazl have been the interlocutors of choice for militants engaging with the Pakistani state. Fazl-ur-Rehman helped negotiate the government's peace deals with TNSM militants between 2005 and 2007. In the government's peace talks with the TTP in 2013–14, the Taliban selected Sami-ul-Haq for its negotiating committee. The rhetoric used by both Sami and Fazl and their parties—the JUI-S and JUI-F—gives license to the Taliban. And Sami and Fazl are in the mainstream in Pakistan, in the media and on the street.

Both parties are also vehemently anti-American. Following American airstrikes on the Afghan Taliban in October 2001, Fazl-ur-Rehman and Sami-ul-Haq led virulent anti-American protests in Pakistan, calling for jihad against America (in response, Fazl was placed under house arrest by General Pervez Musharraf).[6] The protesters chanted along: "Death to America." Six years later, the Pakistan Taliban would use similar rhetoric to turn against the Pakistani state.

Sami-ul-Haq currently leads the Difa-e-Pakistan Council (the Defense of Pakistan Council, DPC), an umbrella organization of forty Islamist and conservative political groups, including militant organizations such as LeT. The DPC was formed after November 2011, when a NATO attack accidentally killed twenty-four Pakistani soldiers. Its platform protests the NATO supply route to Afghanistan that runs through Pakistan, U.S. drone strikes, and trade with India. The vice president of the council is none other than Hafiz Saeed, the leader of the LeT. The leader of the Jamaat, Siraj-ul-Haq, is the secretary general. The DPC shows how anti-Americanism, anti-India sentiment, and Islamism unite these political Islamists with extremists.

Yet there is also a divide between the militants and the Islamists. For one, political Islamists recognize the legitimacy of the Pakistani state and the electoral system; extremists reject these notions. Their views on violence also separate the two. Their rhetoric is similar, but extremists essentially use violence to try to achieve the ideological goals of Islamists—such as imposing Sharia and purging Pakistan of foreign and secular influences—while Islamists shun violence.

Taliban attacks on Islamists make the seams between Islamists and militants clear. The Pakistan Taliban attacked a Jamaat-e-Islami rally in 2010, killing twenty people; it killed two former JUI-F Members of the National Assembly (MNAs) in separate attacks; and it has attacked Fazl-ur-Rehman three times—twice in 2011 and once in 2014, the *maulana* (title denoting Islamic scholar) narrowly escaping each time. When the TTP attacked Fazl in 2014, it claimed: "We very proudly claim responsibility for the suicide attack on Fazl-ur-Rehman and we will do it again. He has been speaking and acting against us, for which he was targeted."[7]

But Fazl was reluctant to name the Taliban as his attacker. Instead he, like Pakistan's mainstream politicians, indulged in conspiracy theories, saying after the second attack in 2011: "Who is behind these attacks? I don't know. I am opposing drone attacks, criticizing the release of Raymond Davis and U.S. policies and raising voice for the release of Aafia Siddiqui, which are not acceptable to some people."[8]

The Islamists' electoral and political experience is instructive. To this end, it is worth looking at the 1977 and 2002 elections in detail, when the Islamists did relatively well electorally. In January 1977, three Islamist parties joined forces with six parties from across the political spectrum to form the Pakistan National Alliance (PNA) in opposition to Bhutto's incumbent Pakistan People's Party.[9] The alliance vowed to bring *Nizam-e-Mustafa* (the Order of the Prophet) to Pakistan. It campaigned in mosques. In addition to

Islamic laws, it promised a just Islamic economic and social order, capitalizing on those who were disenchanted with Bhutto's industrial and labor reforms. Support for the PNA was, thus, only partly religious; it was also economic. The alliance benefited from an anti-incumbent platform at a time of increasing unpopularity for Bhutto.

The Jamaat-e-Islami emerged as the most successful of the PNA's constituent parties, and was in a position to dominate the alliance.[10] But the PNA won only thirty-six out of 216 seats in the March 1977 election, while the Pakistan People's Party (PPP) won 155 seats. The PNA argued the election was rigged; JI activists led large demonstrations against the results.

In response, Bhutto attempted to appease the PNA by giving in to some of its demands. He banned alcohol and nightclubs, made Friday a national holiday, and heralded Sharia as the law of the land. But Zia imposed martial law on July 5, 1977, three months after the election, not allowing the PNA any time in the opposition—and removing Bhutto, thus rendering his political concessions futile.

The second time Islamists did well electorally was in 2002, in an election that was anything but ordinary. The JI, the JUI-F, the JUI-S, and three other Islamist parties joined together to form a political party, the Muttahida-Majlis-e-Amal (MMA).[11] A former head of the ISI, Hamid Gul, engineered the alliance. The MMA rode on Musharraf's meddling with the election to benefit himself. Musharraf disqualified the two major political parties' leaders (Nawaz Sharif and Benazir Bhutto) through a new law that two-term prime ministers could not run for election again. He also mandated that legislators needed at least a bachelor's degree to run for parliament—cutting off the National Assembly from 97 percent of the population and a third of incumbent legislators—but not from Islamists, whose religious degrees he granted equivalence to bachelor's degrees.[12]

The MMA alliance campaigned with the old Nizam-e-Mustafa slogan, combining it with a virulent anti-Americanism—"it is a war between Islam and the American infidel"—that resonated widely in Pakistan after the U.S. invasion of Afghanistan in 2001.[13] The Election Commission of Pakistan assigned a book as the MMA's election symbol—of great significance in Pakistan where illiterate voters rely on party electoral symbols to vote. The MMA promptly equated the book with the Quran, saying that a vote for them would be a vote for the Quran. In a season of severely restricted campaigning for the other parties, the MMA was allowed to run a full campaign in mosques and madrassas.

The alliance won fifty-nine of 272 seats nationally, and also did well provincially, leading the provincial government in the North West Frontier Province and a coalition government in Baluchistan from 2002 to 2007. Fazl-ur-Rehman was the leader of the MMA and led the opposition in parliament during most of the 2002 to 2007 election term.

The actions of the MMA while in power are revealing. The party did not leave much of a legal impact, although it did block reforms. In the NWFP, the MMA-dominated provincial assembly unanimously passed a Shariat bill soon after it began its term; however, the provincial government failed to meet its own provisions—to set up educational and economic commissions to Islamize schooling and the economy in the province.[14] This was part of a larger pattern of legal actions never completed by the MMA government; Islamic bills were introduced and committees were set up but they ended up ignored or tabled. According to Joshua White, "Many of the [MMA's] most outlandish proposals came from the Nifaz-e-Shariat Council, a quasi-governmental recommendatory body set up by the MMA which debated the establishment of a 'vice-and-virtue ministry' within the provincial government. . . . Almost without exception, the Council's recommendations were announced with fanfare, featured prominently in the local press, and then promptly and studiously ignored."[15]

The MMA also introduced a *hisba* (accountability) bill in 2005. Some of the bill's provisions were superfluous given existing laws.

But its most controversial initiative was to set up the office of a *mohtasib*, a religious ombudsman to whom citizens could report un-Islamic behavior.[16] Pakistan's Supreme Court knocked the bill down.

Eventually realizing that legal Islamization would be elusive, the MMA turned to a populist agenda and began focusing on social and economic reforms. The Islamists focused on girls' education in the NWFP, working with donors including the U.K.'s Department for International Development (DfID) and the World Bank. At the same time, the Islamists also channeled discretionary funds to religious madrassas.[17]

In all, the MMA government in NWFP did have a negative impact on society and norms. Music was banned on public transport. Vigilantes blacked out billboards with pictures of women. Rather than overt laws, the government would "signal to business proprietors such as owners of wedding halls, managers of video stores, and local musicians that certain behaviors were no longer 'appreciated' in the province."[18] Pashtuns, and not just liberal ones, grumbled about such changes. Perhaps realizing this, the MMA never wrote them into law.

In the federal government, the MMA blocked reforms on women's issues and on curricula. When the federal government tried to reduce the number of Islamic verses in the government school curriculum in 2005, the MMA objected and the decision was reversed. But political Islamists have been able to have this kind of impact—especially on the education system—even without significant electoral power.

Where the MMA wreaked the most damage was vis-à-vis the growing militancy in NWFP that was able to consolidate itself during the MMA's time in power (2002–07). The MMA did not support the TNSM's violent actions (in Fazl-ur-Rehman's words: "It has never been MMA's policy to use force to implement Islam"[19]), although members from its ranks certainly had connections with and sympathies for these militants. But in ignoring it and dealing with the insurgents passively, the MMA empowered the militants' organization and gave them space to expand. Hassan Abbas quotes a politician from Swat, Mohammad Ayub Khan, at a public rally in Swat: "[the] MMA is responsible for terrorism in Swat. It overlooked terrorists' camps and their explosive-laden vehicles in Swat."[20]

Ultimately the MMA was constrained by its own weaknesses—the longstanding rivalry between its two main parties, the Jamaat-e-Islami and the Jamiat Ulema-e-Islam Fazl, and the dominance of "its military patrons," which left it "vulnerable to manipulation by the state."[21] The alliance broke up after one term in power. In the 2008 election, Islamists reverted to a negligible number of seats in the National Assembly and were booted out of power in the NWFP in favor of the secular Awami National Party.

Islamist parties are not a monolith, and treating them as such misses an essential element of Islamist politics in Pakistan. They typically espouse different interpretations of Islam. They compete with one another for votes. Their MMA alliance came to provincial power only under exceptional circumstances—and the meddling of a military government—and did not last beyond one term. They moderated their policies when voters pushed back on them, and their frictions with each other lowered the collective strength of their alliance.

The influence of Islamists cannot be divorced from the civilian-military-political equation in Pakistan. Both the civilians and the military rely on Islamists—the military uses them as a pawn against the mainstream civilian parties (as it did with the PNA), and the civilians use them as a crutch. But the question is whether Pakistan's main political parties have overestimated the political strength of the Islamists, surrendering to their demands on the Ahmadi laws, as Bhutto did, and caving in to their agitation against reform of madrassas and the public curriculum, and changes to the blasphemy law, as leaders have done since the 1990s. Given the Islamists' lack of success electorally and their relative ineffectiveness while in power, could mainstream politicians call their bluff? It seems those politicians fear the street power of Islamists, thinking they need them for legitimacy, and defer to their coalition building power. Yet Islamists need the validation of a coalition, too, and it would appear that mainstream politicians still have the upper hand, if only they were to use it.

Islamists exercise a direct control over society, even apart from the pressure they exert via the state. This extends beyond their time in power (during which the MMA affected societal norms and freedoms in the NWFP). In a recent example, in March 2017, the Jamaat's student wing, the IJT, attacked an ethnic Pashtun cultural event at Punjab University, touting it as un-Islamic; five students were injured in the clash. Islamists, thus, strong-arm society to mold it to their liking. Thanks to the concessions the state makes to them, they feel they have the power to do so.

We should be clear that Islamism does not imply extremism; the two are distinct. Islamist parties are nonviolent, and they recognize the legitimacy of the Pakistani state and the electoral system; extremists reject these notions. Yet, as I have discussed, there are links between Islamists and extremists, ranging from ex-Islamist extremists to current Islamists who are clearly militant group sympathizers. And the rhetoric and narratives of extremists and Islamists overlap. In Pakistan, a society that sees Islamist narratives in the mainstream, this blurs the lines between support for political Islamists and sympathy for the extremist cause.

MADRASSAS

Pakistan's endemic poverty, widespread corruption, and often-ineffective government create opportunities for Islamist recruitment. Poor education is a particular concern. Millions of families, especially those with little money, send their children to religious schools, or madrassas. Often these schools are the only opportunity available for an education, but some have been used as incubators for extremism.

—*The 9/11 Commission Report*[22]

The Numbers and the History

Madrassas as a phenomenon are neither new nor unique to Pakistan—Islamic religious seminaries existed pre-partition in the Indian subcontinent and still exist in India today; they are found in countries from Morocco to Indonesia. Pakistan's religious seminaries, as we know from chapter 2, served the manpower and ideology that fueled the anti-Soviet jihad in Afghanistan in the 1980s. During this time, sources suggest, the number of madrassas grew exponentially. According to Mariam Abou-Zahab, "mosques and deeni [religious] madrassas with sectarian affiliations were built everywhere, often on state lands."[23] Haroon K. Ullah says that the number of madrassas in Pakistan tripled between the mid-1970s and mid-1990s.[24]

In the years after 2001, the popular press and various scholars floated a set of estimates of madrassa numbers and enrollments, mainly based on interviews with government officials, who in turn based these on conjecture rather than on surveys or census numbers. The numbers were commonly pegged at 10,000 madrassas and 1 million enrolled madrassa students, but there was some variation in the enrollment estimates: between 500,000 and 2 million students. The numbers of madrassas were, at times, quoted in the tens of thousands.

As mentioned in the previous chapter, academics Tahir Andrabi, Jishnu Das, and Asim I. Khwaja have largely debunked the numbers on madrassa enrollment and prevalence. According to the 1998 census (Pakistan's most recent one to date), 159,225 students were enrolled in madrassas. Using a different data source—multiple rounds of the Pakistan Integrated Household Survey—the authors estimate between 151,000 and 178,000 children enrolled in madrassas across the years 1991, 1998, and 2001.[25]

They also used the National Educational Census of 2005 to show that only 7 percent of Pakistani villages have a madrassa and that 4 percent of the population lives in villages where the only schooling option is a madrassa.[26] The data show relatively higher madrassa prevalence in Khyber Pakhtunkhwa (KPK), and especially in the districts near Waziristan. In KPK, 13 percent of villages have a madrassa; in the seven districts near Waziristan, 33 percent of villages have madrassas (as of 2005). Seven percent of the population in KPK and 17 percent of those in the districts near Waziristan live in villages where madrassas are the only school option.[27]

Thus the vast majority of Pakistanis are not in the position of madrassas being their only schooling choice; in fact, just the opposite. Where there are other choices, the authors say, the poor are not more likely to attend madrassas than those better off: "In settlements where other schooling options exist, less than 1 percent of all enrolled children go to madrassas and this fraction is the same for all income groups." Where there are no choices other than madrassas, "the fraction of children going to madrassas increases and is higher among the poor compared to the rich (although it stays below 4 percent for all income groups). Nevertheless, the biggest difference between these two types of settlements is not the increase in the use of madrassas but the dramatic decline in overall enrollment. Thus, though the share of madrassas increases, this is offset by a sharp reduction in the size of the overall enrollment pie."[28]

It is worth noting that Andrabi and his coauthors' numbers likely are an underestimate. The National Education Census includes only registered madrassas, while there are probably many more unregistered ones. Also, as mentioned in the previous chapter, data on enrollments from the household surveys and national census are based on individual self-reports. The data do not include people who attend or attended madrassas part-time while enrolled primarily in a public or a private school—likely a significant number. Yet the evidence all points to significantly smaller numbers of madrassa enrollments than others have presumed.

The authors also find that, of households that have at least one child enrolled in a madrassa, 75 percent send their second (and/or third) child to a public or private school (or both). They argue that this within-household variation in the schooling decision means that household-level characteristics, like religiosity or fundamentalism, or even access to schooling options, are not the key to the decision to send children to madrassas, countering the usual narrative about such households.

Andrabi and his coauthors do show suggestive, quantitative evidence of a link between the Afghan war and madrassas. People born between 1974 and 1978 were more likely to report having a religious education than those before; and this continued for those born between 1979 and 1983, the last cohort for which the authors have a complete educational history.[29]

While madrassa numbers are not what they have been pegged to be, it is certainly true that some madrassas, such as Sami-ul-Haq's Dar-ul-Uloom Haqqania in Akora Khattak, are incubators for extremism. And we know that students vie for its spots. Each year more than 18,000 children compete for only 500 available spaces. The madrassa teaches 1,500 boarding students and a thousand day students, ages six and up.[30]

Enrollment numbers are only one aspect of the story. The influence of madrassas in Pakistan is linked to their problematic, unregulated curricula and the reach of their graduates, many of whom go on to become clerics at mosques and Islamic Studies teachers in public schools, thus exercising a far-reaching effect on Pakistan's society and its youth.

Links to Extremism

There are well-documented ties between madrassas and militants that began with the mujahideen connection and continue today.

Sufi Muhammad, the head of the TNSM, was once an Afghan mujahid—he was schooled at a "disreputable" madrassa on the Afghan border.[31] Militant groups and known fundamentalists openly run madrassas in Pakistan. Lashkar-e-Taiba runs a madrassa near Lahore in Muridke, the Markaz-al-Dawah-al-Irshad; the infamous Lal Masjid in Islamabad runs madrassas for girls and for boys that indoctrinate students to become jihadis, as shown vividly in a recent documentary, *Among the Believers*. Tashfeen Malik, one of the San Bernardino attackers, attended al-Huda, an institute for Islamic education for women (she also attended a mainstream university); she is the only known militant with an al-Huda background.

The majority of madrassas do not have terrorist ties. But given that the madrassas that indoctrinated students in jihadist ideologies during the Afghan jihad still exist, and given that they have not shed that ideology, it is obvious that some madrassas will continue to create militants. Peter Singer puts the percentage of madrassas with militant links at 10 to 15 percent of the total.[32] A Pakistani newspaper reports that of the almost 14,000 madrassas in Punjab in 2015, nearly 300 have links to terrorist activity.[33]

In 2012, Pakistan's Federal Investigation Agency (FIA) published a list of its 230 most wanted terrorists. I looked at their educational backgrounds to examine the links between madrassa education and militancy in Pakistan. Of the 230 listed terrorists, the FIA has the education backgrounds of seventy. Of these seventy, sixty have some form of mainstream education—primary, middle, or secondary school—as their main educational background, while nine have a religious education alone. Three more have some religious education that is not their primary educational background. One is listed simply as literate.

Therefore, 17 percent of the terrorists for whom we have educational information have some form of madrassa education. This percentage is higher than the proportion of madrassa enrollees in the overall Pakistani population (which we can discern from Andrabi and others' work)—implying that terrorists are somewhat more likely to have madrassa links than the general population does.

Most of these terrorists have a mainstream education. Yet as we know from the previous chapter, mainstream education does not radicalize directly (though it does set up a framework for students that fits in neatly with extremist views, and it does not prepare students to counter militant propaganda). Madrassa education has a much more direct link with radicalization, especially in those madrassas that indoctrinate their students in a jihadi mindset—but this radicalization does not necessarily imply violence.

Madrassa Curriculum and Attitudes

The content of madrassa education is not uniform. Registered madrassas belong to one of five boards in Pakistan—four of which correspond directly to sects or sub-sects of Islam (Deobandi, Barelvi, Shia, Ahl-e-Hadith) and one to the political party Jamaat-e-Islami. The roots of the Deobandi and Barelvi boards go back to madrassas founded as part of the Islamic revival in nineteenth-century India; the Deobandis fundamentally oppose sufi or "folk" Islam and its central concept of intercession by saints; the Barelvis subscribe to this notion. The Ahl-e-Hadith (sometimes referred to as Salafi or Wahhabi) is the most puritanical of the South Asian sub-sects of Islam; Markaz-al-Dawah-al-Irshad, the LeT's madrassa in Muridke, is an Ahl-e-Hadith seminary.[34] The funding of Pakistani madrassas is mostly private: they are funded via charity, remittances, and also reportedly through funding from foreign sources, particularly Saudi Arabia for Ahl-e-Hadith madrassas and Iran for Shia madrassas. The Pakistani government at times helps with funding and support in terms of providing land: Saleem Ali says that 90 percent of madrassas in Islamabad are built on state land.[35]

Little is known about the curriculum of unregistered madrassas, and while the curriculum of registered madrassas also varies

133

significantly, we know more about what is taught in them. For the first few years they attend a madrassa, students typically learn to read the Quran and memorize it. Later they follow the *Dars-e-Nizami* curriculum, an eight-year course that covers the biography of the Prophet, the Quran, the Hadith (the sayings of the Prophet), logic, rhetoric, Arabic grammar and literature, and jurisprudence.[36] Texts date to the fourteenth century. The style of teaching is regimented and based on rote memorization. We should note two things: an increasing number of madrassas teach "modern" subjects like math and science in addition to religious teaching; and just because someone has some madrassa education doesn't mean he is a madrassa graduate or that he has gone through the entire Dars-e-Nizami curriculum—he can be a dropout, having, say, memorized only part of the Quran.

Madrassas are by definition sectarian because they teach their own sect's interpretation of Islam. In terms of what else is taught, studies that have reviewed various madrassa textbooks provide more information, although these are non-random, and thus non-representative, studies. It seems that jihadi literature is taught at madrassas, but much of it is not publicly available.[37] Madrassas emphasize refuting beliefs that are seen as "heretical" to Islam—for instance, the Jamaat-e-Islami's 2002 syllabus includes four books that refute the beliefs of Ahmedis alone.[38] We can piece together that anti-West and anti-India sentiment is taught at madrassas. As Tariq Rahman reports: "The Jamaat-e-Islami probably goes to great lengths—judging from its 2002 syllabus—to make its students aware of Western domination, the exploitative potential of Western political and economic ideas, and the disruptive influence of Western liberty and individualism on Muslim societies."[39]

A study by the United States Commission on International Religious Freedom (USCIRF) that reviewed madrassa textbooks notes the intolerance toward religious minorities in these texts, and the depiction of non-Muslims as not equal to Muslims. The worst treatment in the textbooks is reserved for *murtads* or apostates, Muslims who have turned away from Islam: one textbook "instructs the reader that such a person must be arrested and taken into the custody of the Muslim state, where he/she is given three days to return to Islam on pain of death. The person who puts this *murtad* to death, even if it be during the three days of reflection (i.e., an extra-judicial execution), is not to be subject to prosecution."[40] Another textbook advocates that apostates be killed on the spot.

In the madrassa textbooks studied by USCIRF, violent jihad is portrayed as the responsibility of individuals, without a need for adjudication by a national government or military. This is clearly problematic, both in terms of a violent notion of jihad and in the sense that it is incumbent upon individuals, and therefore can be operationalized by would-be militants and vigilantes.

Saleem Ali notes article titles from the newsletters of the madrassa at Binori town in Karachi that document an intolerant sectarianism and virulent anti-West rhetoric: one article, from 1999, was titled "What is the apostasy of Shias?"; another, from 1998, titled "The world's largest assemblage of hypocrites is the United Nations" argued that the UN is worthy of jihad against it because of its betrayal of the Taliban.[41]

These kind of intolerant, extremist curricula—present at least in some madrassas—affect student attitudes. According to a survey conducted by Tariq Rahman in Pakistan's major cities in 2002 and 2003, madrassa students have more extreme attitudes on an array of issues relative to students with a mainstream education, whether in public or in private schools. Rahman's survey is based on a small sample size and nonrandom selection—it should not be considered conclusive, but it is certainly suggestive. Madrassa students seem to be more supportive of jihad than public or private school students: 53 percent of madrassa students said they would support jihadi groups to fight against the Indian army to take back Kashmir from India, while 33 percent of matric students and 22 percent of O-level students said they would do so.[42] Madrassa students are also more likely to advocate open war against India over Kashmir than other students—60 percent of madrassa students said they supported war against India relative to 40 percent of matric students. Only 34 percent of madrassa students said they would support resolving the Kashmir issue through peaceful means, while over 70 percent of matric and O-level students said they would do so.

Madrassa students are also far less likely to support equal rights for minorities than public and private school students. Only between 10 percent and 20 percent of madrassa students supported equal rights for Ahmadis, Christians, and Hindus, while near majorities of matric students supported equal rights for Ahmadis and Hindus, and 66 percent supported equal rights for Christians.

Other studies also show that madrassa students exhibit "extreme" attitudes. Saleem Ali cites an Institute of Policy Studies survey from 2002 that shows that 82 percent of Deobandi madrassa students interviewed favored the Taliban as their role model for Islamization in Pakistan—a striking illustration of their conformity with extremists.[43] His own interviews with madrassa students revealed an anti-Americanism not based on a generalized anti-West sentiment for most respondents, but driven by the more proximate issue of civilian casualties caused by the United States during combat, especially in Iraq and Afghanistan.[44]

Madrassa Regulation

Madrassas occupy a particular place in Pakistan's education system as centers for religious education in an Islamic republic; even the director of the government's Madrassa Education board referred to them as "the fortress of Islam."[45] In the words of a madrassa leader quoted by Saleem Ali: "it is we madrassas who are keeping the Islamic values and traditions intact for hundreds of years. If the religious schools had not been there, Islam and [the] society of so-called Muslims would have faced irreparable losses at the hands of liberals and Western agents."[46] That explains why Pakistan's madrassas are resistant to reform and regulation, even to registration.

To win over the ulema in the 1970s, Prime Minister Zulfikar Ali Bhutto offered to grant the highest madrassa degrees equivalence to university degrees; Zia made this a reality in the 1980s. But by the late 1990s, there was a sense that the madrassa sector needed regulation given its exponential growth in the 1980s. Musharraf started the process of looking into madrassa reform soon after he came to power in 1999. The Madrassa Education board was founded in 2001 to "mainstream" madrassas, and along with it, three "model" madrassas were created that combined religious teaching with contemporary subjects. In 2002, Musharraf introduced the Voluntary Madrassa Registration and Regulation Ordinance that aimed to register all madrassas and prevent the teaching of radical material. The ulema and Islamists vehemently resisted the reform, rendering it unsuccessful. In 2005, Musharraf tried his hand at implementing the ordinance again. Sami-ul-Haq, the leader of the JUI-S, railed against it, arguing that it was a capitulation to foreign pressure. In a speech at a convention in Islamabad in May 2005, Sami said: "The international community is against only one thing, the seminaries or madrassas. Its target is not the Islamic army, the Muslim rulers, generals or the politicians. It is not concerned with our natural resources. Its target is only one— to label our seminaries as hub[s] of terrorism and extremism."[47] According to the International Center for Religion and Diplomacy, only 10 percent of madrassas complied with the registration ordinance.[48] In 2007, reform plans for the madrassa sector were shelved, the Ministry of Education having spent only $4 million of the $100 million that the government had allocated for the reform since 2001.[49]

Madrassas are not as pervasive in Pakistani society as many have claimed. Yet some madrassas are clearly linked with militancy, and many indoctrinate their students in intolerance. The influence of these madrassa graduates infiltrates Pakistani society through the mosques they lead and the students they teach as Islamic Studies teachers in public schools. Madrassas must, thus, be regulated, but given their self-identification as bastions for the preservation of Islam against Western influence in Pakistan, that is not an easy task. Islamists are the first-line defenders of madrassas against regulation and stand squarely in the way of reform. The state lacks the political will to take them on, due in no small part to its own ideological tethering to religion.

We have seen that political Islamists do not necessarily warrant the power the Pakistani state accords to them. Correcting for that overestimate, and an ideological realignment of the state, will be necessary for Pakistan to move forward with madrassa reform. At the same time, the state can make it clear that it will not threaten all madrassas, only extremist ones; it can make moderate madrassas a partner in its push for regulation and reform.

SIX

An Appraisal and a Way Forward

February 2017 brought a brutal few weeks, one attack after another in a rapid succession that left Pakistan reeling. The Tehrik-e-Taliban Pakistan (TTP), its breakaway Jamaat-ul-Ahrar (JuA), and ISIS claimed responsibility. Of course, terrorist attacks had continued in 2015 and 2016, but there were fewer of them, and more time between them; the TTP's strength seemed to have abated with the army's Zarb-e-Azb operation, and it led the country to believe it was winning its war against terror. That was the official line. But it betrayed what the state doesn't understand, or won't admit: the difference between terrorism and extremism, that killing terrorists and dismantling their networks goes only so far. As long as an extremist, jihadist ideology remains intact, militants will reincarnate with a renewed ferocity, and they will show that they can still sow terror. And so they did.

On February 13, a suicide bomber blew himself up at a protest in front of the provincial assembly on Lahore's majestic Mall

Road, killing at least fourteen; the JuA claimed responsibility. On Thursday, February 16, two attacks in Mohmand and in Dera Ismail Khan in the northwest killed five people each, and were claimed by JuA and TTP, respectively. Most devastating was an attack the same day on Sehwan Sharif, the famed shrine of the Sufi saint known as Lal Shahbaz Qalandar in Sindh, where more than eighty people died as they joined together in a devotional dance called *dhamaal*, among them many women and children. Hundreds were injured. ISIS claimed responsibility.

Lal Shahbaz Qalandar's actual name was Syed Muhammad Usman Marwandi; *Lal Shahbaz* literally means the *Red Falcon*, and *Qalandar* means *ascetic*. In a *New York Times* op-ed after the attack, Fatima Bhutto, a granddaughter of Zulfiqar Ali Bhutto, evoked the essence of Sehwan, its "red and green fairy lights," the "men in flowing robes and long dreadlocks," its air filled with the scent of roses "sold in small plastic bags."[1] That Sehwan was targeted on a Thursday was deliberate. Thursday evenings were special at Sehwan. Crowds gathered to listen to devotional Sufi music called *qawwalis* and to dance in a dhamaal; men, women, and children together. They came not only on Thursday but every day of the week, at all times, traveling long distances to pray and to pay their respects to their venerated saint.

The inclusiveness and tolerance of Sufi Islam is reflected in Sehwan—it welcomes people of all faiths and encompasses the rituals of other religions. Sufi Islam and its music and dance are firmly South Asian, and draw from the region's non-Islamic traditions. They are, thus, perceived as heretical by the puritan purveyors of Wahhabi Islam.

Lal Shahbaz Qalandar was honored in a *qawwali*, "Dam Mast Qalandar," that has become as famous as the man:

O laal meri pat rakhio bala Jhoole Laalan
Sindhri da, Sehwan da, sakhi Shahbaz Qalandar
Dama dam mast Qalandar

This translates to:

> *O red-robed, protect me always, Jhoole Lal*
> *Friend of Sindh, of Sehwan, generous*
>   *Shahbaz Qalandar*
> *Every breath intoxicated by you, Qalandar*

Qawwali is notable for its lyrics evoking love and the intoxication of love. The qawwal sings about this in relation to Allah and the Prophet Muhammad, but in words that the non-religious can interpret as referring to romantic love. The music has universal appeal, attracting even those who do not understand the words. As an NPR reporter described it: "The songs build slowly in speed and intensity, swelling up to ecstatic heights. Listeners are swept up in that lyrical and musical potency, dancing, clapping and singing along. Qawwali is very much a communal experience that can last for hours. . . . It is, for its performers and audiences, a conduit for experiencing the divine."[2]

On June 22, 2016, Pakistan's most famous qawwali singer, forty-five-year-old Amjad Sabri, was gunned down in Karachi. He was on his way to participate in a morning show on TV, where he was a fixture that Ramadan, singing qawwalis, moving the hosts and the audience to tears, sometimes crying himself, as he sang. Sabri's family had been singing for generations, rumored to go all the way back to a Mughal emperor's court. He was the only Sabri descendant still singing.

The TTP's Hakimullah Mehsud group claimed responsibility for Sabri's assassination, saying it killed him for blasphemy. In 2014, the Islamabad High Court had summoned Amjad Sabri and Geo TV, one of Pakistan's leading television channels, for blasphemy, citing Sabri's qawwali on a morning show and a reference the show's hosts had made to the Prophet's family.

Sabri's killing and the attack on Sehwan close the loop between Pakistan's laws, its narrowing constraints of acceptable religious practice, and terrorism. Terrorist groups are able to directly call on Pakistan's own laws to justify their attacks on Pakistani citizens.

The attack on Sehwan is only the most recent in a string of attacks on Sufi shrines since 2005. In 2016, the Hazrat Shah Noorani shrine was attacked in Baluchistan, killing at least fifty-two during a dhamaal. ISIS claimed responsibility. On a Thursday night in 2010, two suicide bombers attacked the 1,000-year-old Data Ganj Baksh shrine in Lahore. Thousands of devotees were at the shrine at the time; more than forty-two people died in the attack. In 2009, terrorists struck the Rahman Baba shrine in the northwest. In 2005, Barri Imam was attacked in Islamabad; twenty died.

The reaction after Sehwan was swift and strong. Prime Minister Nawaz Sharif said it was an attack on the progressive and inclusive future of Pakistan. "The Sufi people predate Pakistan's history, and played an important part in the struggle for its formation," he said. "An attack on them is a direct threat to Jinnah's Pakistan and will be dealt as such."[3] The army chief was quoted as saying: "Each drop of the nation's blood shall be revenged, and revenged immediately. No more restraint for anyone."[4] Both men visited Sehwan the day after the attack.

Post-Sehwan, the army launched its first countrywide counter-terror operation (previous terror operations had been geographically focused in the northwest). The army named this operation ominously, as usual, calling it *Radd-ul-Fasaad*, which literally means to rid Pakistan definitively of all trouble. It killed more than a hundred terrorists in the days immediately afterward but revealed few details on those targeted. Despite its swift response, the state downplayed the rise of ISIS in Pakistan, and the director general of the Inter-Services Public Relations (ISPR), the army's public relations wing, alluded to conspiracies and pointed the finger to Afghanistan and India. "Recent terrorist acts are being executed on directions from hostile powers and from sanctuaries in

Afghanistan. We shall defend and respond."[5] According to *Newsweek Pakistan*: "Local media has found its boogeyman: India. Whether claimed by Pakistani Taliban offshoot Jamaat-ul-Ahrar or the Islamic State militant group, they say, the attacks were perpetrated by terrorists based in Afghanistan, whose intelligence agency retains close ties with India. As such, they maintain, these attacks are intended to destabilize Pakistan enough to make it forget Kashmir."[6] In the short term, some even argued that these attacks were intended to cancel a highly anticipated cricket game, the final of the Pakistan Super League in Lahore (the game did take place amid heightened security).

And while hundreds protested in outrage and grief after Sehwan and blamed the state, ordinary citizens also murmured about how visits to shrines and dhamaal were un-Islamic. Thus the ordinary Pakistani ventured into casual, dangerous *takfirism*—accusations against other Muslims of apostasy deserving death—their indoctrination in evidence.

The loop between terrorism, the narrowing bounds of religion, and Pakistan's laws was completed in another way. Pakistan's own citizens justified terrorist attacks against their fellow countrymen—and they could call on the blasphemy laws and an extreme interpretation of their religion, validated by the Pakistani state, for justification.

In chapter 3, I described Lahore in December 2016, festive with Christmas trees and decorations for the new year. That month in Islamabad, the government officially launched a Christmas peace train. In those months, Prime Minister Nawaz Sharif frequently invoked Jinnah's Pakistan (Quaid *ka* Pakistan) as his progressive vision for Pakistan, and spoke of its future as a modern democracy, a peaceful, economically vibrant nation. But that is easier said than done, and his own government's actions pandered to the right just days after reassuring the left, taking one step back even as they took one forward.

To put that in sharp relief, it is worth recounting some of the events of those few months. In December 2016, Sharif officially recognized Pakistan's first Nobel Prize winner, the physicist Abdus Salam. Salam, who should have been Pakistan's pride, had been sidelined in life and in death in his own country because he was an Ahmadi. Sharif designated scholarships in his name and named the physics department of the Quaid-e-Azam University after him. This was a bold step. Then in March, Pakistan's parliament for the first time passed a law recognizing Hindu marriages. Nawaz Sharif celebrated Holi with Karachi's Hindu community in March 2017, inviting a prompt fatwa against him from fundamentalists. At least publicly, perhaps superficially, the government tried to reassure religious minorities that it recognized them and would protect their rights.

On the other hand, the state was stamping down on secular dissent in a systematic way. In early January 2017, five bloggers, online activists who had been advocating for a secular Pakistan, "were disappeared." Although no one knows for certain, their absences fit the pattern of enforced disappearances allegedly undertaken by Pakistan's clandestine intelligence agencies. The bloggers had been critical of the country's clerics, the military, and religious extremism. Most of them were not nationally known figures, but the best known of them was a poet and a professor who had been critical of the military's repression in Baluchistan. There was a liberal outcry about their disappearances and they turned up after a few weeks, silenced. Meanwhile, an online smear campaign began against them for being associated with groups posting overtly blasphemous content online—it is unclear whether these connections were real or not. In any case, the message was clearly sent: dissent against the Pakistan project was dangerous and could land you with a charge like blasphemy, akin to a death sentence in Pakistan.

After this episode, the state's rhetoric around blasphemous content on social media became increasingly charged. Interior

Minister Chaudhry Nisar Ali Khan publicly engaged in chest thumping and emotional exhortations against social media accounts accused of insulting the religion and announced action against them. It is no coincidence that this government clampdown coincided with increased vigilante and mob violence against those accused of blasphemy; in the most brazen and shocking of these attacks, on April 15, 2017, Mashal Khan, a twenty-three-year-old student at Abdul Wali Khan University in Khyber Pakhtunkhwa, was killed for alleged blasphemy by a frenzied mob of his fellow students on campus. He was a self-described "humanist," a journalism student whose social media posts revealed progressive, liberal values. The mob, in its hysteria, called his posts anti-Islam.

The state views those who argue for a secular Pakistan to be more of a threat than fundamentalist cleric Abdul Aziz or Lashkar-e-Taiba head Hafiz Saeed; in the state's perspective, the former corrupt the Pakistan project. The perverse outcome is that the Pakistani establishment clamps down on forms of secular dissent more than Islamist overreach or militancy. The ability and the will to push back on this impulse by the civilian government will define Pakistan's future.

The National Action Plan (NAP) that reflects Pakistan's current counterterror and counterextremism policy is a twenty-point list released after the Peshawar Army Public School attack of December 2014 (see box 6-1). As is obvious, the plan mixes counterterror and counterextremism policy, and what could be called preventing violent extremism policy. It has come to embody the set of national expectations from the state in the fight against extremism, but it is little more than a list, without specifics, mixing actions and outcomes. Lost in the national focus on the NAP is the fact that Pakistan had a detailed National Internal Security Policy (NISP) that preceded it—and while the NISP honed in on coordinating security policy alone, and less on preventing and countering extremism, it did so well, through outlines for coordinated

---

BOX 6-1   **Twenty Points of the National Action Plan**

1. Implementation of death sentence of those convicted in cases of terrorism.
2. Special trial courts under the supervision of Army. The duration of these courts would be two years.
3. Militant outfits and armed gangs will not be allowed to operate in the country.
4. NACTA [National Counter Terrorism Authority], the anti-terrorism institution, will be strengthened.
5. Strict action against the literature, newspapers, and magazines promoting hatred, extremism, sectarianism, and intolerance.
6. Choking financing for terrorist[s] and terrorist organizations.
7. Ensuring against re-emergence of proscribed organizations.
8. Establishing and deploying a dedicated counterterrorism force.
9. Taking effective steps against religious persecution.
10. Registration and regulation of religious seminaries.

(continued)

---

actions at the provincial and national levels (via measures such as a rapid response force, for example). NAP added to the NISP by introducing military courts and fast tracking executions of terrorists, and adding a number of "soft" measures to counter hate and extremist rhetoric in the media and in madrassas and mosques.

But the National Action Plan has been problematic on multiple levels—in terms of intent and narrative, as well as implementation. The narrative on the NAP is half-baked and surrounded by a vacuum—it acknowledges that hate and extremist rhetoric are problematic, but the narrative remains silent on the roots of

11. Ban on glorification of terrorists and terrorist organizations through print and electronic media.
12. Administrative and development reforms in FATA with immediate focus on repatriation of IDPs.
13. Communication network of terrorists will be dismantled completely.
14. Measures against abuse of internet and social media for terrorism.
15. Zero tolerance for militancy in Punjab.
16. Ongoing operation in Karachi will be taken to its logical end.
17. Balochistan government to be fully empowered for political reconciliation with complete ownership by all stakeholders.
18. Dealing firmly with sectarian terrorists.
19. Formulation of a comprehensive policy to deal with the issue of Afghan refugees, beginning with registration of all refugees.
20. Revamping and reforming the criminal justice system.

Source: National Counter Terrorism Authority Pakistan (NACTA), "20 Points of National Action Plan" (http://nacta.gov.pk/NAPPoints20.htm).

terrorism and extremism in Pakistan, and how these relate to the country's own policies. The NAP acknowledges extremism in Pakistan, but treats it as an issue that the state had no role in creating. It does not tackle the negative repercussions of Pakistan's ideological construct and, as a corollary, takes no issue with Pakistan's own laws, its public education system, or its subscription to and use of the notion of jihad.

An analysis of major Pakistani television talk shows from January 2015, the month after the Peshawar attack and immediately after the National Action Plan was announced, is telling.[7] It shows that on the topic of security, some of the main items discussed included the "army chief's strategy to eliminate terrorism," "banning of madrassas and Jamaat-ud-Dawa," and "foreign involvement in terrorism." Thus even immediately after the Peshawar attack, in the short phase of clarity that it brought, the idea of foreign involvement in terrorism remained significant. And the notion that fighting terrorism is the military's domain also reveals the sense that countering terror was perceived as a mainly kinetic issue, one the military could deal with by fighting—by corollary, a problem without deep social roots in the country.

The implementation of the NAP began, it seemed, relatively earnestly; but then became sporadic, and in 2017 it has been hard to see any action on some of the soft measures at all. In keeping with an early push for implementation under the NAP, the government took action against hate rhetoric in mosques and literature in madrassas. In October 2015, the government announced it had arrested over 9,000 preachers for spreading hate; in November of the same year, it said it had sealed over 100 religious seminaries for "stoking sectarianism."[8] There were also reports of mosque loudspeakers shut down, madrassas raided, and hate material seized through 2015. Thousands of madrassas were "geotagged"—their locations identified, presumably to make them easier to track down and regulate. But there was little sense of how systematic this was; and reports of all this stopped somewhat abruptly after the end of 2015. Yet even that year, militant literature and propaganda continued to be clearly available in urban Pakistan. In the spring of 2015, my research assistant was able to obtain Lashkar-e-Taiba magazines from its shop in the inner city of Lahore; among these was the *Al-Harmain* magazine from July 2014, which included an article celebrating ISIS and its victories in Iraq.

Other key elements of the NAP have also been blatantly disregarded, as evidenced in the army's treatment of a former Taliban militant who appears to have been granted some measure of immunity in exchange for giving up arms and sharing intelligence. This terrorist, Ehsanullah Ehsan, was the spokesman of the Pakistan Taliban and its more brutal offshoot, Jamaat-ul-Ahrar, and is one of those responsible for the Peshawar Army Public School attack of December 2014 and dozens of others. The army has paraded him in front of the media and let him make a public confession, allowing him to be presented in a sympathetic light. Ehsan "confessed" that India's intelligence agencies have been supporting the Taliban. It is a narrative that perfectly suits the Pakistan army and the one for which it wants airtime. This directly violates point eleven of the NAP—a ban on the glorification of terrorists in the media—and is not the only instance of a violation.

What, in the end, makes the Pakistani case unique? Intolerance and other extreme attitudes do not, in themselves, differentiate Pakistan from other contexts—not from India, where anti-Pakistan sentiment is rampant, nor from other conflict-ridden places where hatred is nurtured. Anti-Muslim violence has risen in the last year in India, perpetrated by Hindu extremists. One can also look to the rise of a xenophobic far right in Western Europe and the United States in the past few years to find displays of a jingoistic nationalism, and even calls to violence among fringe elements. States other than Pakistan have biased textbooks—India, Israel, and China—and indoctrinate their students in an explicitly nationalistic narrative, as well.

The difference between these contexts and Pakistan—at least so far—lies in the role played by the Pakistani state and its official institutions, which validate not only paranoia and hatred but also violence in the name of religion. The Pakistani state points the finger at its eastern neighbor for the terror that strikes it. The army justifies its wars as jihad and uses the jihadi narrative to support militants behind the scenes. The state's support of violence in the name of religion extends to a pass for ordinary citizens who respond violently—based on the country's blasphemy laws and anti-Ahmadi laws—to perceived religious intransigence by their fellow citizens. This means cases of vigilante and mob violence that go unprosecuted, with the notable exception of Mumtaz Qadri's case.

How much of this was inevitable? Could Pakistan have gone down a different path? In retrospect, we can rationalize the impulses and the imperatives faced by the Pakistani state, leading to the actions it took. Faced with a larger, stronger neighbor, and the religion-based cause for partition, it is understandable that Pakistan ended up this way. Pakistan's training of the mujahideen to fight in Afghanistan, its support of Kashmiri jihadist groups, its passive response to the Pakistan Taliban, its internal reliance on religion as a source of unity while stamping down on ethnic differences, its circumscribing of the boundaries of religion—these decisions have their root in the same thing: the insecurity felt from India and the willingness to use religion or religious ideology as a weapon to counter it. After all, Islam was the most readily available, natural unifier for a country created for Muslims. Some circumstances that Pakistan faced were not in its control—for instance, the Soviet invasion of Afghanistan. Yet at each point, Pakistan could have taken steps that defied its fundamental sense of insecurity, the desire to achieve parity relative to India, and the impulse to reach for and to misuse religion. They may have been harder to take, but there were always other options.

Those who puzzle over the different paths India and Pakistan took despite the countries' shared history and people need only look back at the varying pressures faced by the two nations at their inception. India did not need to define itself on the basis of something new—its nationalism was secure and secular, based on territory and centuries of history. It sought strength from the diverse ethnicities and languages of its population (although it has faltered on religious tolerance at times and much more notably recently, invoking Hindu nationalism and marginalizing its Muslims, it has retained its political commitment to a secular polity). It was the larger and more powerful neighbor—and had the advantage of starting off with the infrastructure and institutions of its history. Pakistan, because it was the one that broke off, started from scratch and was economically vulnerable and politically ill-defined. It had to justify its existence, for which it relied on the crutches of religion and enmity with India. Pakistan's initial vulnerability is a part of its national narrative and one that it uses to validate its sense of victimhood. It is this vulnerability that led to the long-term dominance of its military, the strongest institution Pakistan inherited.

It is the military's dominance and, ultimately, a single military ruler, General Muhammad Zia-ul-Haq, who proved the most harmful for Pakistan. Zia faced the same imperatives others had faced before him and responded along similar lines—but with a difference of degree and with a disproportionate strong-handedness that was partly personality driven and partly driven by the fact that he exercised absolute power. It is not that those before him were free of blame. Prime Minister Zulfikar Ali Bhutto was the one who declared Ahmadis to be non-Muslims. Pakistan's first constitution in 1956 put in place enabling and repugnancy clauses that were the precursors of an Islamization of society and the legal system, respectively. But were it not for a fundamentalist military dictator, Pakistan would not have seen its particular blasphemy laws and would not have seen the strategic use of jihad. It would have been a different place.

Zia's time was a dark one for Pakistan. The day he was killed in a plane crash in 1988, liberal and moderate homes across the country, repressed by his eleven years of rule, toasted to a new day for Pakistan and to a brighter future without his iron grip. In the months after that, there was an overwhelming sense of relief, of possibility. Yet the effect of the seeds Zia had sown continued to haunt Pakistan, and have become fully apparent two decades after his death in the violence afflicting the country. Zia's regime changed the legal, political, and societal course of Pakistan and limited the set of available options for his successors to roll his policies back. This is in part because Pakistan's ideological framework has remained unchanged.

Where does this book leave us? With cautious hope. That the roots of extremism can be so clearly traced to the state absolves Pakistani society of much of the blame (although the state did respond to what it saw were its needs for legitimacy in the eyes of Pakistani citizens); yet now that society is ideologically indoctrinated, a reversal is difficult, and its views have become self-sustaining through generations. We see that regular Pakistanis have become casual takfiris. When combined with a state that cannot control violence and that, at times, condones it, this is alarming. Yet we still see widespread denunciations of terrorist violence by the public.

The major shift for Pakistan must come from its center, although there is a role for its citizenry to play, as well. We have seen subtle, faltering inflection points emerging from the two civilian governments since 2008. Governor Salmaan Taseer, Senator Sherry Rehman, and Religious Minorities Minister Shahbaz Bhatti from the relatively left-leaning Pakistan People's Party government took on the blasphemy law in 2010, but their attempt at reform was thwarted by Taseer and Bhatti's assassinations. Nawaz Sharif was once Zia's protégé, so he is not of a liberal pedigree, but is aware of the need for Pakistan's image to be restored and he recognizes the importance of economic development to that end. He made overtures to India and his government tackled the sectarian group Lashkar-e-Jhangvi by killing its leader Malik Ishaq in a police shootout in July 2015. Yet Sharif has not shown any interest in a deep engagement on institutional reform or on the question of Pakistan's ideological direction. The cast of characters around him—his interior minister and others—are the same that presided over his conservative terms in the 1990s and have shown little imagination. His interior minister Chaudhry Nisar, in particular—who presided over NAP—is sympathetic to Islamists.

Sharif's political position was precarious through the first seven months of 2017, as he was mired in a Supreme Court case on his family's unexplained assets, news of which had first leaked via the Panama papers in April 2016. On July 28, 2017, Pakistan's Supreme Court disqualified him from office in the wake of a joint investigation team's incriminatory report on the lack of a satisfactory explanation about his family's acquisition of assets. In the end, the court's reasoning was based on a relative technicality. It ruled that because Sharif had not declared his foreign employment or salary in his nomination papers in 2013—although the salary was tagged at AED10,000 (United Arab Emirates dirhams) but not withdrawn—he violated article 62 1(f) of the constitution that requires that a member of the National Assembly be honest. Corruption cases against him were referred to the National Accountability Bureau; an accountability court is to rule on them within six months. Sharif insists he will fight the Supreme Court's decision and the corruption cases against him. The long-term impact of the disqualification remains to be seen, but this weakens the cause of democratically elected governments, at least in the short term, in Pakistan.

Nothing less than a conscious ideological shift—a shedding of both the insecurity felt from India and the repressive nature of its commitment to religion—will ultimately change the course for Pakistan. This does not mean a renunciation of religion—but Pakistan can now redefine its nationalism without the crutch of religion. In 2017, Pakistani patriotism is a given; the new country felt threatened in 1947 when the provinces that constituted Pakistan had no common thread other than religion, but now they have a shared history and love for their country that can drive nationalism. A new generation also need not feel the insecurity from India and the enmity toward it to buy into the Pakistan project. Pakistan can, instead, look to a positive narrative based on being a modern democracy, as I argued in a recent blog article, titled *Redefining Pakistan*—and it can begin this now by investing in economic advancement and political development.[9] The resolution of the civilian military equation in favor of the civilians is the only chance for such an ideological shift for Pakistan.

The discarding of the insecurity paradigm will weaken the hold of the country's military, which is precisely why it pushes back on it. The army did not respond kindly to Nawaz Sharif's overtures to India's Prime Minister Narendra Modi. India's hawkishness, especially during right-wing Bharatiya Janatiya Party–led governments, also makes it difficult for Pakistan to justify its shedding of the all-consuming defensive posture vis-à-vis India. When Modi mentioned Baluchistan in his Independence Day speech in 2016, decrying the Pakistani state's repression of the insurgency there, it raised alarm bells in Pakistan. When Indian politicians talk about Akhand Bharat (literally an undivided India, that includes Pakistan and Bangladesh) and when Afghanistan and India seem close, Pakistan's fears of Indian encirclement come to the fore.

It is unclear whether the military's dominance will break. Democratic regimes are more stable than ever before in the country's history, and the military has shown a reticence to get involved in the day-to-day matter of governing. Yet the military continues to run a tight ship on security matters, benefiting from the sense that it is the only organization competent to do so. Civilians will have to demonstrate that they are up to the task if they are to eventually assume control over security policy. The military also tolerates no criticism against itself, muzzling dissent, equating it with a lack of patriotism. And because it weakened the most powerful political party in Pakistan, Nawaz Sharif's disqualification will strengthen the army.

In shifting its narrative, Pakistan must first self-examine. It needs to have an open, honest discussion about extremism, acknowledge the link with its own policies, and to treat extremism as a consequence and as a symptom of its ideological direction. In the near term, to counter extremist propaganda, it must painstakingly separate its own narrative from that of extremists. As I have shown, on some counts it is difficult to separate the two: the Pakistan

Taliban argues, for example, that it wants to impose Islamic law on the country; Pakistani citizens, schooled in the "ideology" of Pakistan, think that goal matches the reason for Pakistan's creation. But Pakistan, while an Islamic republic, is no theocracy; as its constitution makes clear, it is a Muslim democracy. The state should school its citizens in its constitution. And it need not be the only one to lead this conversation. Pakistan's influential media can play a role, too.

Pakistan must also have an honest conversation about the interpretations of Islam that relate to extremism and the elements in its legal system that foment it. The infiltration of Saudi-inspired puritan Islam is a culprit, as are its own blasphemy and anti-Ahmadi laws that define and criminalize religious out-groups (those deemed irreligious, as it were). The blasphemy law does this nebulously, and society has used it to get to ever-narrowing definitions of what makes a proper Muslim, and what constitutes "pure" forms of Islam and Islamic practice. This makes it difficult for Pakistanis to denounce terrorist attacks that target those cast as irreligious.

The blasphemy law is here to stay, at least for the foreseeable future—yet changes to the law, or additions to it that blunt its misuse, can be made. The most urgent of these would be to make false accusations of blasphemy punishable, and harshly so. Sherry Rehman's 2010 bill had proposed this, and the Supreme Court argued this in its ruling on Qadri. The death penalty for blasphemy should also be taken off the table. To be feasible, the argument for blasphemy law reform will have to be made in religious terms. An activist group of citizens can lead the call for such reform in much the same way as women's rights groups led the call for reform of Pakistan's women's laws, but they will have to do so less publicly given that the blasphemy issue is much more fraught than that of women's rights. The state will have to participate in equal measure.

More generally, Pakistan must make it clear that no citizen and no non-state institution has a right to adjudicate religiosity.

Ideally, not even the state, but that will prove difficult in a state that in its requirements for members of parliament requires that they have "adequate knowledge of Islamic teachings" and practice "obligatory duties prescribed by Islam."[10]

Islamists will oppose such legal reforms, as they oppose reforming public school curricula and regulating madrassas. But the Pakistani state can reevaluate its relationship with Islamist parties. Given Islamists' political unpopularity and their internal divisions, along with their ineffectiveness and relative moderation while in power, it appears the state has overreacted to them. Islamist parties, it turns out, did not warrant their status as the most potent pressure force on the state; it must now rein them in. In this, the state can exploit the divisions within Islamists.

The Pakistani state can no longer obfuscate and point fingers at its neighbors and the West. Letting go of conspiracy theories will be hard, as they suit Pakistan's political class. But analytical thinking via an improved education system will enable the citizenry to counter conspiracy theories on its own. This will not be an easy thing to teach, since critical thinking runs against the country's non-questioning culture, one that allows those in positions of authority to define information. That culture, in turn, helps the spread of conspiracy theories. Cass Sunstein and Adrian Vermeule argue that conspiracy theories spread in "informational cascades," where individuals in a tight group rely on the judgment of others to form opinions when they cannot seek out the information themselves[11]—easier to do in a hierarchical culture. As the information spreads, each successive individual knows more people that espouse the theory, so he accepts it as well.

Sunstein and Vermeule also argue that conspiracy theories are particularly difficult to counter because of their "self-sealing quality"; attempts to counter the theory are considered conspiracies themselves. A government attempt to directly counter these theories is likely to be unsuccessful for a variety of reasons: due to distrust of the state; because countering the theory publicly may lead to a further spread of the theory, since it is repeated and hence legitimized in a public space; and because the state is often the conspiracy entrepreneur in the first place, as in Pakistan. Citizens may thus prove more effective at countering conspiracy theories than the state.

In Pakistan, it is not a single theory that must be countered, but a web of interconnected narratives that feed off each other. If Pakistani schools start teaching their students how to acquire and critically evaluate multiple sources of information, students will be able to counter false information. If schools focus on analytical thinking that emphasizes logic over a single theory or answer, that will also help. We need not look to government schools alone for this. Low-cost private schools that now provide education to a third of the country's students can commit to such an approach. The private sector can take a lead on this by creating an alternative board of education that certifies secondary school degrees based on this alternate style of education, thus deemphasizing the government board exams.

Beyond introducing critical thinking, Pakistan must revamp its public education for a new generation and un-indoctrinate its citizens. As I mentioned in chapter 4, Pakistan's younger generations are broadly more favorable toward terrorist groups than its older generations, and if its education sector does not change, the country will continue to trend toward more extreme views. Getting more students to and through school will not be the only answer, as we have seen, though it will improve attitudes on terrorist groups (but not until university on India and the United States). Curricula, in particular related to Pakistan Studies, must change. There are some simple, and relatively noncontroversial, steps the state can take immediately to improve curricula: introduce world history as a core subject; replace its own biased, exclusionary Pakistan Studies textbooks with parallel O-level textbooks; encourage classroom discussion and debate.

On madrassa reform and regulation, the government can use moderate madrassas as a partner and as an example. This will help counter the frequent criticism that madrassa reform fulfills a Western agenda and is a recipe for Western influence to infiltrate Pakistan's society.

Finally, the Pakistani army will have to let go of religious justifications for war. And anti-India and sectarian militants must go. We know that militant foot soldiers migrate across groups with different objectives and new incarnations like ISIS can count on different stripes of jihadists for outsourcing. There needs to be zero tolerance on militancy for this to end.

The Pakistani state's motivations for this realignment—of its "ideology," of its laws, on militancy, in its education system—must be seen as internal, not external, which would be a nonstarter and would be widely derided and opposed by both opposition political parties and citizens. For Pakistan, making these changes would not be caving in to foreign influence; rather, it would own them, as their first benefits would fall to it. And given that a perceived negative American influence serves to sustain Pakistan's conspiracy-laden narratives, any American attempt to directly affect policy on these issues will only be counterproductive.

Yet there are ways the United States can exert influence on the Pakistani state behind the scenes, to incentivize and encourage it to take steps—say, to improve its curriculum, to treat its minorities better, to amend its blasphemy laws—that will serve Pakistan's long-term interests as well as help American security interests. For far too long, America has pressured Pakistan to do the things that prioritize America's short-term security gains over Pakistan's long-term ones. America has used the Pakistani military as its security partner, preferring its predictability and strength to the greater uncertainty of working with Pakistan's civilian governments. In the process, it has propped up the military, which, I have argued, has harmed the country.

The relationship is dysfunctional and needs a reset. Pakistan is untrusting, perceives that America looks out only for itself, and fears U.S. withdrawal from the region and a drying up of American aid. It keeps up appearances for America while maintaining its own policies. The double game is played out in the open. America signals its displeasure, yet continues to give Pakistan aid. The relationship rumbles along.

A change in paradigm would benefit both countries. America should make it clear that it will reward Pakistan's own social, educational, and legal reforms, not just a fulfillment of American interests, and that it will do so by treating Pakistan with dignity and with a seat at the table—the way Pakistan thinks America treats India and other emerging powers. More than anything, Pakistan craves respect and importance. America can make it clear that it can offer that in recognition of the internal changes Pakistan makes. America must also commit to upholding and strengthening Pakistan's democracy rather than its military.

Development aid to Pakistan, say to help build more schools, may be a mixed bag in terms of security outcomes, at least with the country's current curricula. We know that more years of education do not necessarily improve views of the United States, although they do improve views on terrorist groups. But evidence shows that unconditional emergency aid does win hearts and minds.[12] Conditional aid also invites backlash and may stoke anti-Americanism. Given this, it will be best to disentangle American development aid from security outcomes. Focusing on directing aid toward the quality of education rather than increasing access alone will also help.

Attitudes matter. As Krueger puts it: "Terrorism occurs within a social context. People are encouraged or discouraged to participate in terrorism by friends, family, co-workers, neighbors, and other associates."[13] The reality is that only a tiny percentage of individuals actually become radicalized enough to commit violence—so looking at violent extremism is a much more random enterprise than understanding attitudes, and attempts at prediction about such extremism based on individual or societal characteristics have limits. But attitudes tend to be widespread and can be explained and understood. I hope to have done so here for the Pakistani case.

Pakistan went through dozens of terrorist attacks while I was writing this book. Each has been devastating for those who wish more for the country, not only because of the death and devastation, but also for the death of an idea—that of a progressive Pakistan; for the reactions of its other citizens; for what is considered justified and what is not; for what can be traced to Pakistan's own policies; for what was preventable. The human toll has been heart wrenching to witness, as has the normalization of extremism in Pakistan.

Yet there is a way out. Not through simple military operations, but through a deeper, conscious realignment. It may seem difficult now, but go back seventy years, to 1947, and imagine that Pakistan took the alternate path at each juncture where it had a choice— between pluralism and exclusion, between openness and a defensive posture. It would have been a different place.

It can change course yet.

APPENDIX A

The Objectives Resolution

Whereas sovereignty over the entire universe belongs to Allah Almighty alone and the authority which He has delegated to the State of Pakistan, through its people for being exercised within the limits prescribed by Him is a sacred trust;

This Constituent Assembly representing the people of Pakistan resolves to frame a Constitution for the sovereign independent State of Pakistan;

Wherein the State shall exercise its powers and authority through the chosen representatives of the people;

Wherein the principles of democracy, freedom, equality, tolerance and social justice as enunciated by Islam shall be fully observed;

Wherein the Muslims shall be enabled to order their lives in the individual and collective spheres in accordance with the teachings and requirements of Islam as set out in the Holy Quran and the Sunnah;

Wherein adequate provision shall be made for the minorities to freely[1] profess and practice their religions and develop their cultures;

Wherein the territories now included in or in accession with Pakistan and such other territories as may hereafter be included in or accede to Pakistan shall form a Federation wherein the units will be autonomous with such boundaries and limitations on their powers and authority as may be prescribed;

Wherein shall be guaranteed fundamental rights including equality of status, of opportunity and before law, social, economic and political justice, and freedom of thought, expression, belief, faith, worship and association, subject to law and public morality;

Wherein adequate provisions shall be made to safeguard the legitimate interests of minorities and backward and depressed classes;

Wherein the independence of the Judiciary shall be fully secured;

Wherein the integrity of the territories of the Federation, its independence and all its rights including its sovereign rights on land, sea and air shall be safeguarded;

So that the people of Pakistan may prosper and attain their rightful and honored place amongst the nations of the World and make their full contribution towards international peace and progress and happiness of humanity.

Source: Constitution of Pakistan, Annex: The Objectives Resolution, article 2A (www.pakistani.org/pakistan/constitution/annex .html).

APPENDIX B

Levels of Education

Table B-1. *Education, 1998 Census*

Completed education level (years of education)	1998 Census
Below primary (<5)	18.30
Primary (5)	30.14
Middle (8)	20.90
Matric (10)	17.29
Intermediate (12)	6.97
Bachelor's (14 year equivalent)	4.38
Master's (16 year equivalent)	1.58
Other (including diploma/certificate)	0.85

Source: Pakistan Bureau of Statistics, "Population Census 1998: Educated Population by Level of Education," Islamabad, Pakistan: Government of Pakistan (1998) (www.pbs.gov.pk/sites/default /files//tables/EDUCATED%20POPULATION%20BY%20 LEVEL%20OF%20EDUCATION.pdf).

Table B-2. *Education of Pew Global Attitudes Survey Respondents, 2013*

Completed education level	Percent
No school	40.6
1–5	14.6
6–8	10.4
9–10	19.0
11–12	7.1
13+	8.3

Source: Author's graph, using Pew Research Center's Global Attitudes Spring 2013 survey data for Pakistan (www.pewglobal.org/datasets/2013/).

Notes

Preface

1. Author's calculation using data from the South Asia Terrorism Portal (www.satp.org/satporgtp/countries/pakistan/database/casualties .htm. Retrieved on February 10, 2016. Data updated as of February 7, 2016).

2. See, for example, Dexter Filkins, "Pakistan's Monster," *The New Yorker*, January 22, 2016.

Chapter 1

1. I use the 2013 data here because the nonresponse rate is at its lowest in 2013, 4 percent. The latest numbers available, for 2015, are surprising—they show a much lower percentage of people who think such violence is never justified (66 percent), though this is after the December 2014 Peshawar school attack that hardened opinions against terrorist groups. It is unclear whether this is a one-time fall or reflective of a trend.

2. The sample was selected through multi-stage cluster probability sampling. For the years with sample sizes of around 1,200, margins of error are 3 percent to 4 percent. For the years 2002, 2007, and 2010,

when sample sizes are around 2,000, margins of error are 2 percent to 3 percent.

3. Pew covers all areas except FATA, Gilgit-Baltistan, Azad Jammu and Kashmir, and areas of instability in Khyber Pakhtunkhwa (formerly the North West Frontier Province), and Baluchistan.

4. The 2003 data was not nationally representative and is not used. Pew fielded two surveys in 2011—one in the spring, and one following the May raid that killed Osama bin Laden in Abbottabad, Pakistan. I mainly use data from the May 2011 survey, as recommended by Pew.

5. The survey was carried out by SEDCO (Socio-Economic Development Consultants, Islamabad, Pakistan), with the questionnaire developed by PIPA.

6. Interviews were conducted across sixty-four primary sampling units in rural areas and thirty-six in urban areas; ten respondents were surveyed in each sampling unit (PIPA reports that the sampling error for a sample of this size is approximately +/– 3.2 percentage points). Baluchistan was oversampled; therefore sampling weights are utilized in the analysis.

7. This question also shows very negative views toward the Taliban (72 percent unfavorable, 6 percent favorable, 23 percent nonresponse) in 2015.

8. Graeme Blair and others, "Poverty and Support for Militant Politics: Evidence from Pakistan," *American Journal of Political Science* 57, no. 1 (January 2013): 30–48, doi:10.1111/j.1540-5907.2012.00604.x. Their experiment asked a control group of respondents about their views of an otherwise neutral policy; the treatment group was told, in addition, that a militant organization of interest "endorsed" the policy. Using the difference in policy support between the treatment and control groups, they could identify average, group-level support for the militant organization of interest (individual-level support cannot be derived from such surveys, which is a detriment).

9. Tahir Andrabi and Jishnu Das, "In Aid We Trust: Hearts and Minds and the Pakistan Earthquake of 2005" (The World Bank Policy Research Working Paper Series 5440, 2010). The authors found that earthquake aid had a lasting effect on trust in foreigners in Pakistan.

10. Some of the material in this section is adapted from my November 2013 column, Madiha Afzal, "On Pakistani Anti-Americanism," *The Express Tribune*, November 14, 2013 (http://tribune.com.pk/story/631495/on-pakistani-anti-americanism/).

11. John Lancaster and Kamran Khan, "Extremists Fill Aid Chasm After Quake," *The Washington Post*, October 16, 2005, sec. World (www.washingtonpost.com/wp-dyn/content/article/2005/10/15/AR2005101501392.html).

12. C. Christine Fair, Neil Malhotra, and Jacob N. Shapiro, "Islam, Militancy, and Politics in Pakistan: Insights From a National Sample," *Terrorism and Political Violence* 22, no. 4 (September 14, 2010): 495–521, doi:10.1080/09546553.2010.492305.

13. The Pew Forum on Religion and Public Life, "The World's Muslims: Religion, Politics and Society," April 2013, Washington, Pew Research Center (www.pewforum.org/files/2013/04/worlds-muslims-religion -politics-society-full-report.pdf).

14. Fair, Malhotra, and Shapiro, "Islam, Militancy, and Politics in Pakistan."

15. Ibid.

16. Anatol Lieven, *Pakistan: A Hard Country* (New York: PublicAffairs, 2012), p. 423.

17. Ibid., p. 437.

Chapter 2

1. Ismail Khan and Salman Masood, "Scores Are Killed by Suicide Bomb Attack at Historic Church in Pakistan," *New York Times*, September 22, 2013 (www.nytimes.com/2013/09/23/world/asia/pakistan-church -bombing.html).

2. Dawn.com, "Peshawar Church Attack an Attempt to Sabotage Taliban Talks: Fazl," September 24, 2013 (www.dawn.com/news /1044903).

3. Dawn.com: Agencies, "Death Toll from Peshawar Church Bombing Rises to 81," September 23, 2013 (www.dawn.com/news /1044846).

4. Khan and Masood, "Scores Are Killed by Suicide Bomb Attack at Historic Church in Pakistan."

5. Zulfiqar Ali, "Drone Strikes Root Cause of Terrorism: Imran," June 25, 2013 (www.dawn.com/news/1020501).

6. Ibid.; Salman Masood and Ihsanullah Tipu Mehsud, "Thousands in Pakistan Protest American Drone Strikes," *New York Times*, November 23, 2013 (www.nytimes.com/2013/11/24/world/asia/in-pakistan-rally -protests-drone-strikes.html).

7. Some of this discussion draws on Madiha Afzal, "The Taliban Is Winning Them Over: Time to Talk to the Pakistani People, Mr. Sharif," *The Brookings Institution*, February 26, 2014 (www.brookings.edu /blogs/up-front/posts/2014/02/26-nawaz-sharif-pakistan-afzal).

8. APP | Dawn.com, "TTP Wants Talks, Calls on Govt to Lead on Ceasefire," February 21, 2014 (www.dawn.com/news/1088539); Nazar Ul Islam, "The Caliphate Cometh," *Newsweek Pakistan*, February 11, 2014 (newsweekpakistan.com/the-caliphate-cometh/).

9. Saud Mehsud, "Pakistani Taliban Say Government Must Embrace Islamic Law," *Reuters*, February 22, 2014 (http://in.reuters.com/article/pakistan-taliban-talks-idINDEEA1L04C20140222).

10. Islam, "The Caliphate Cometh."

11. APP | Dawn.com, "TTP Wants Talks, Calls on Govt to Lead on Ceasefire."

12. Christophe Jaffrelot, *The Pakistan Paradox: Instability and Resilience*, Ceri Series in Comparative Politics and International Studies (Oxford University Press, 2015), p. 80.

13. Ibid., p. 95.

14. Farzana Shaikh, *Making Sense of Pakistan* (Columbia University Press, 2009), pp. 82, 86.

15. Jaffrelot, *The Pakistan Paradox,* pp. 95–96, 109.

16. Shaikh, *Making Sense of Pakistan,* p. 33.

17. Ibid.

18. Mr. Jinnah's Presidential Address to the Constituent Assembly of Pakistan, August 11, 1947 (www.pakistani.org/pakistan/legislation/constituent_address_11aug1947.html).

19. Jaffrelot, *The Pakistan Paradox,* p. 96.

20. Ibid., p. 97.

21. Website of the Pakistan army, "Motto of the Pakistan Army" (https://www.pakistanarmy.gov.pk).

22. Shaikh, *Making Sense of Pakistan,* p. 160.

23. Jaffrelot, *The Pakistan Paradox,* p. 217.

24. Stephen P. Cohen, *The Idea of Pakistan* (Brookings Institution Press, 2006), p. 70. Cohen expands on his notion of Islamic nationalism: "Often personally secular, the Islamist nationalist worldview is shaped by the notion of grievance, not by principles of Islam, although the policies of this group are justified as being supporting of the Muslim Ummah, or community."

25. Steve Coll, *Ghost Wars: The Secret History of the CIA, Afghanistan, and Bin Laden, from the Soviet Invasion to September 10, 2001* (New York: Penguin Books, 2005), p. 61.

26. Ibid., p. 62.

27. Haroon K. Ullah, *Vying for Allah's Vote: Understanding Islamic Parties, Political Violence, and Extremism in Pakistan*, South Asia in World Affairs Series (Georgetown University Press, 2014), p. 93.

28. Coll, *Ghost Wars,* p. 68.

29. Ibid.

30. As cited in C. Christine Fair, Neil Malhotra, and Jacob N. Shapiro, "Democratic Values and Support for Militant Politics: Evi-

dence from a National Survey of Pakistan," *Journal of Conflict Resolution* 58, no. 5 (August 2014): 743–70, doi:10.1177/0022002713478564, p. 747.

31. John Lancaster and Kamran Khan, "Extremists Fill Aid Chasm After Quake," *Washington Post*, October 16, 2005, sec. World (www .washingtonpost.com/wp-dyn/content/article/2005/10/15 /AR2005101501392.html).

32. Steve Coll, "Lashkar-e-Taiba," *The New Yorker*, December 1, 2008 (www.newyorker.com/news/steve-coll/lashkar-e-taiba).

33. Stephen Tankel, "Lashkar-e-Taiba: Past Operations and Future Prospects," New America Foundation: National Security Studies Program Policy Paper, April 2011, p. 9.

34. Hassan Abbas, *The Taliban Revival: Violence and Extremism on the Pakistan-Afghanistan Frontier* (Yale University Press, 2015); Ullah, *Vying for Allah's Vote*, pp. 141–42.

35. Abbas, *The Taliban Revival*, pp. 145–46.

36. Ibid., p. 112.

37. Ian Talbot, *Pakistan: A New History* (Oxford University Press, 2015), p. 194.

38. Abbas, *The Taliban Revival*, p. 148.

39. Pamela Constable, "Islamic Law Instituted In Pakistan's Swat Valley," *The Washington Post*, February 17, 2009, sec. World (www.wash ingtonpost.com/wp-dyn/content/article/2009/02/16 /AR2009021601063.html).

40. Website of the Pakistan army, "Motto of the Pakistan Army" (https://www.pakistanarmy.gov.pk).

41. Ibid.

42. Website of the Pakistan army, "A Journey from Scratch to Nuclear Power" (https://www.pakistanarmy.gov.pk).

43. Ibid.

44. Dawn.com, "1971 'Jihad': Print Ads from West Pakistan," December 16, 2014 (www.dawn.com/news/1151200).

45. Website of the Pakistan army, "A Journey from Scratch to Nuclear Power."

46. John F. Burns, "Nuclear Anxiety: The Overview; Pakistan, Answering India, Carries Out Nuclear Tests; Clinton's Appeal Rejected," *New York Times*, May 29, 1998 (www.nytimes.com/1998/05/29/world /nuclear-anxiety-overview-pakistan-answering-india-carries-nuclear -tests-clinton.html); BBC.com, "World: Monitoring Nawaz Sharif's Speech," May 28, 1998 (http://news.bbc.co.uk/2/hi/world/monitoring /102445.stm).

47. Madiha Afzal, "Pakistan's Democratic Opportunity," *The Cairo Review of Global Affairs*, no. 23 (Fall 2016): 76–85. This paragraph is adapted from my discussion in this article.

Chapter 3

1. "Taseer's Remarks about Blasphemy Law," *The Express Tribune*, January 5, 2011 (http://tribune.com.pk/story/99277/taseers-remarks -about-blasphemy-law/).

2. Associated Press, "Salmaan Taseer's Bodyguard Pleads Guilty to Murder," *The Guardian*, February 14, 2011, sec. World news (www .theguardian.com/world/2011/feb/14/salmaan-taseer-guard-pleads -guilty).

3. Carlotta Gall, "Assassination Deepens Divide in Pakistan," *New York Times*, January 5, 2011 (www.nytimes.com/2011/01/06/world /asia/06pakistan.html).

4. For a longer discussion, see Wajahat S. Khan, "A Generally Bel- licose Society's Antisocial Media: Reporting Murder & Debating God in a Nation at War," Discussion Paper (Joan Shorenstein Center on the Press, Politics and Public Policy at Harvard University, Novem- ber 2011).

5. Gall, "Assassination Deepens Divide in Pakistan."

6. Saeed Shah, "Mainstream Pakistan Religious Organisations Applaud Killing of Salmaan Taseer," *The Guardian*, January 5, 2011, sec. World news (www.theguardian.com/world/2011/jan/05/pakistan -religious-organisations-salman-taseer).

7. Omar Waraich, "Pakistan's Pols Paralyzed by Religious Extrem- ism," *Time*, January 13, 2011 (http://content.time.com/time/world /article/0,8599,2042522,00.html).

8. Gall, "Assassination Deepens Divide in Pakistan."

9. Aoun Sahi, "Barelvi Form," *The News International, Pakistan*, August 7, 2011 (http://jang.com.pk/thenews/aug2011-weekly/nos-07 -08-2011/spr.htm#4).

10. Saeed Shah and Qasim Nauman, "Pakistanis Throng for Funeral of Man Hanged for Killing Critic of Blasphemy Laws," *Wall Street Jour- nal*, March 1, 2016, sec. World (www.wsj.com/articles/pakistanis -throng-for-funeral-of-man-hanged-for-killing-critic-of-blasphemy-laws -1456855688).

11. Ibid.

12. Mehreen Zahra-Malik, "Footprints: Mumtaz Qadri Mosque, Memorials to Our Misdeeds," May 11, 2014 (www.dawn.com/news /1105513).

13. Agencies | Dawn.com, "Pro-Qadri Protesters Given the Night to Disperse on Their Own: Nisar," March 29, 2016 (www.dawn.com/news /1248676).

14. Geo News, "Negotiations Successful: Protest Leaders Announce End to Red Zone Sit-In," March 30, 2016 (https://www.geo.tv/latest/103126-Sit-in-to-end-peacefully-today-PM-directs-meeting).

15. Dawn.com, "Timeline: Accused under the Blasphemy Law," September 19, 2012 (www.dawn.com/2012/09/19/timeline-accused -under-the-blasphemy-law/).

16. Farzana Shaikh, *Making Sense of Pakistan* (Columbia University Press, 2009), p. 87.

17. Ibid., p. 85.

18. Christophe Jaffrelot, *The Pakistan Paradox: Instability and Resilience*, The Ceri Series in Comparative Politics and International Studies (Oxford University Press, 2015).

19. Seyyed Vali Reza Nasr, *The Vanguard of the Islamic Revolution: The Jama'at-i Islami of Pakistan*, Comparative Studies on Muslim Societies 19 (University of California Press, 1994), p. 131.

20. See the Constitution of 1956, Article 198 (http://pakistanspace.tripod.com/archives/56_12.htm).

21. Ibid., Article 197.

22. The amendment added that the Advisory Council would examine all existing laws "with a view to bringing them into conformity with the teachings and requirements of Islam as set out in the Holy Quran and Sunnah" and to advise the National Assembly, a provincial assembly, the president, or a governor on any question on "whether a proposed law is or is not repugnant to the teachings and requirements of Islam as set out in the Holy Quran and Sunnah."

23. See the Constitution of Pakistan, Articles 19 and 20 (www.pakistani.org/pakistan/constitution/part2.ch1.html).

24. Ibid., article 22.

25. Human Rights Watch, "Pakistan: Massacre of Minority Ahmadis" (New York: Human Rights Watch, June 1, 2010) (https://www.hrw.org /news/2010/06/01/pakistan-massacre-minority-ahmadis).

26. Added by the Second Amendment Act of 1974 (49 of 1974), Section 2 (with effect from September 17, 1974) (www.pakistani.org /pakistan/constitution/amendments/2amendment.html): "A person who does not believe in the absolute and unqualified finality of The Prophethood of Muhammad (Peace be upon him), the last of the Prophets or claims to be a Prophet, in any sense of the word or of any description whatsoever, after Muhammad (Peace be upon him), or recognizes

such a claimant as a Prophet or religious reformer, is not a Muslim for the purposes of the Constitution or law."

27. Zia replaced Bhutto's article with this (www.pakistani.org /pakistan/constitution/orders/po24_1985.html):

a) "Muslim" means a person who believes in the unity and one- ness of Almighty Allah, in the absolute and unqualified finality of the Prophethood of Muhammad (peace be upon him), the last of the prophets, and does not believe in, or recognize as a prophet or religious reformer, any person who claimed or claims to be a prophet, in any sense of the word or of any description what- soever, after Muhammad (peace be upon him); and (b) "non- Muslim" means a person who is not a Muslim and includes a person belonging to the Christian, Hindu, Sikh, Buddhist, or Parsi community, a person of the Qadiani Group or the Lahori Group who call themselves "Ahmadis" or by any other name or a Bahai, and a person belonging to any of the Scheduled Castes.

28. See the full text of these clauses (www.pakistani.org/pakistan /legislation/1860/actXLVof1860.html).

298-B. Misuse of epithets, descriptions and titles, etc., reserved for certain holy personages or places:

(1) Any person of the Qadiani group or the Lahori group (who call themselves "Ahmadis" or by any other name who by words, either spoken or written, or by visible representation: a) refers to or addresses, any person, other than a Caliph or com- panion of the Holy Prophet Muhammad (peace be upon him), as "Ameer-ul-Mumineen," "Khalifa-tul-Mumineen," "Khalifa-tul- Mumineen," "Sahaabi or "Razi Allah Anho"; (b) refers to, or addresses, any person, other than a wife of the Holy Prophet Muhammad (peace be upon him), as "Ummul-Mumineen"; (c) refers to, or addresses, any person, other than a member of the family "Ahle-bait" of the Holy Prophet Muhammad (peace be upon him), as "Ahle-bait"; or (d) refers to, or names, or calls, his place of worship a "Masjid"; shall be punished with imprisonment of either description for a term which may extend to three years, and shall also be liable to fine.

(2) Any person of the Qadiani group or Lahori group (who call themselves "Ahmadis" or by any other name) who by words, either spoken or written, or by visible representation refers to the mode or form of call to prayers followed by his faith as "Azan," or recites Azan as used by the Muslims, shall be punished with

imprisonment of either description for a term which may extend to three years, and shall also be liable to fine.

298-C. Person of Qadiani group, etc., calling himself a Muslim or preaching or propagating his faith: Any person of the Qadiani group or the Lahori group (who call themselves "Ahmadis" or by any other name), who directly or indirectly, poses himself as a Muslim, or calls, or refers to, his faith as Islam, or preaches or propagates his faith, or invites others to accept his faith, by words, either spoken or written, or by visible representations, or in any manner whatsoever outrages the religious feelings of Muslims shall be punished with imprisonment of either description for a term which may extend to three years and shall also be liable to fine.

29. Farahnaz Ispahani, *Purifying the Land of the Pure: Pakistan's Religious Minorities* (Noida: HarperCollins Publishers India, 2015), p. 148.

30. Ibid., p. 158.

31. Ibid., p. 157.

32. Ibid., pp. 151–52.

33. Ibid., pp. 152–53.

34. Issam Ahmed, "Why Taliban Attacks Two Muslim-Minority Mosques in Pakistan," *Christian Science Monitor*, May 28, 2010 (www.csmonitor.com/World/Asia-South-Central/2010/0528/Why-Taliban-attacks-two-Muslim-minority-mosques-in-Pakistan).

35. Waqar Gillani and Jane Perlez, "Attackers Hit Mosques of Islamic Sect in Pakistan," *New York Times*, May 28, 2010, sec. World / Asia Pacific (www.nytimes.com/2010/05/29/world/asia/29pstan.html).

36. Mohammed Hanif, "Why Pakistan's Ahmadi Community Is Officially Detested," BBC.com, June 16, 2010 (http://news.bbc.co.uk/2/hi/programmes/from_our_own_correspondent/8744092.stm).

37. Shaikh Aziz, "A Leaf from History: Zia's Referendum," *Dawn*, August 2, 2015 (https://www.dawn.com/news/1197376).

38. 298-A. Use of derogatory remarks, etc., in respect of holy personages:

Whoever by words, either spoken or written, or by visible representation, or by any imputation, innuendo or insinuation, directly or indirectly, defiles the sacred name of any wife (Ummul-Mumineen), or members of the family (Ahle-bait), of the Holy Prophet (peace be upon him), or any of the righteous Caliphs (Khulfa-e-Rashideen) or companions (Sahaaba) of the Holy Prophet (peace be upon him) shall be punished with imprisonment of either description for a term which may extend to three years, or with fine, or with both.

39. See Pakistan Penal Code (www.pakistani.org/pakistan/legislation /1860/actXLVof1860.html).

40. Ibid.

41. Beena Sarwar, "Sherry Rehman's Proposed Bill to Amend Offences Relating to Religion," *Journeys to Democracy*, December 16, 2010 (https:// beenasarwar.com/2010/12/16/sherry-rehman's-proposed-bill-to-amend -offences-relating-to-religion/).

42. Karin Brulliard and Shaiq Hussain, "World," *The Washington Post*, March 3, 2011, sec. World (www.washingtonpost.com/wp-dyn /content/article/2011/03/01/AR2011030101394.html).

43. BBC.com, "What are Pakistan's Blasphemy Laws?" November 6, 2014 (www.bbc.com/news/world-south-asia-12621225).

44. United States Commission on International Religious Freedom, "Pakistan Annual Report" (Washington: U.S. Commission on International Religious Freedom, 2016).

45. "Judgement in Criminal Appeals No. 210 and 211 of 2015" (Supreme Court of Pakistan, October 2015).

46. Ibid.

47. Ibid.

48. Non-Muslims could not testify or argue in the Shariat courts. The rulings of the provincial Shariat benches could be appealed at the Shariat Appellate bench of the Supreme Court.

49. No Shia judges were appointed to the Federal Shariat court, leading to opposition.

50. The Pew Forum on Religion and Public Life, "The World's Muslims: Religion, Politics and Society," April 2013, Washington: Pew Research Center (www.pewforum.org/files/2013/04/worlds-muslims -religion-politics-society-full-report.pdf).

Chapter 4

Note: Sections of this chapter draw heavily on my previous articles on the subject, including "A Failed Curriculum Reform," *Express Tribune*, January 15, 2014 (http://tribune.com.pk/story/659111/a-failed-curriculum -reform); "Education and Attitudes in Pakistan: Understanding Perceptions of Terrorism," Special Report (United States Institute of Peace, April 2015); "Making 'O' Levels Pakistan Studies Textbooks Available to All," *Express Tribune*, February 2, 2016 (https://tribune.com.pk/story /1038923/making-o-levels-pakistan-studies-textbooks-available-to-all); and "Dissimilar Histories: History Curricula in Government and Elite

Private Schools," in *Routledge Handbook on Contemporary Pakistan*, edited by Aparna Pande (forthcoming 2017).

1. Stephen Philip Cohen, *The Idea of Pakistan* (Brookings Institution Press, 2004), p. 171.

2. Pervez Hoodbhoy and A. H. Nayyar, "Rewriting the History of Pakistan," in *Islam, Politics, and the State*, ed. Asghar Khan (London: Zed Press, 1985), pp. 164–77.

3. Haroon K. Ullah, *Vying for Allah's Vote: Understanding Islamic Parties, Political Violence, and Extremism in Pakistan*, South Asia in World Affairs Series (Georgetown University Press, 2014), p. 86.

4. Hoodbhoy and Nayyar, "Rewriting the History of Pakistan."

5. Hasan Askari Rizvi and others, *Pakistan Studies for Secondary Classes: Class IX–X* (Lahore, Pakistan: Punjab Textbook Board, 2002), p. 262.

6. Muhammad Hussain Choudhary and Uzma Azam, *Pakistan Studies: Class 9* (Lahore, Pakistan: G. F. H. Publishers, 2013), pp. 9–10.

7. Rizvi and others, *Pakistan Studies for Secondary Classes: Class IX–X*, p. 43.

8. Fida Hussain Khokhar, Syed Qavi Ahmed, and M. Rafiq Dhanani, *Pakistan Studies for Classes IX–X* (Jamshoro, Pakistan: Sindh Textbook Board, 2013), p. 15.

9. Rizvi and others, *Pakistan Studies for Secondary Classes: Class IX–X*, p. 10.

10. Choudhary and Azam, *Pakistan Studies: Class 9*, p. 114.

11. Pakistan Bureau of Statistics, Pakistan Social and Living Standards Measurement Survey 2012–2013 (PSLM), 2014, Islamabad: Government of Pakistan Statistics Division (www.pbs.gov.pk/content/pakistan-social-and-living-standards-measurement-survey-pslm-2012-13-provincial-district). The net enrollment ratios are much lower (they measure enrollment at each level for government-specified age groups). The government specifies ages five to nine years for primary, ten to twelve for middle, and thirteen to fourteen for matric; but also calculates net enrollment ratios with ages six to ten for primary, eleven to thirteen for middle, and fourteen to fifteen for matric. Current net enrollment ratios at the primary, middle, and secondary levels are 57 percent, 22 percent, and 13 percent respectively.

12. Tahir Andrabi and others, "Religious School Enrollment in Pakistan: A Look at the Data," *Comparative Education Review* 50, no. 3 (2006), pp. 446–77, doi:10.1086/503885.

13. In my interview with the chairman and senior staff at the Punjab Textbook Board (in October 2013), it was clear they were unhappy

with the paring down of their role given their subject specialists and expertise; they considered the quality of the books written by private publishers to be deficient because of their lack of expertise; incentives for corruption by the government in granting the contract; and profit maximization by the publisher, keeping costs, and therefore quality, low. On the other hand, officials I met at the Curriculum Authority argued that the Textbook Board ran a monopoly and compromised quality.

14. Choudhary and Azam, *Pakistan Studies: Class 9*, p. 40.

15. Ibid., p. 117.

16. Ibid., p. 127.

17. Fazal-ur-Rahim Marwat and others, *Pakistan Studies for Grade IX* (Peshawar, Pakistan: Khyber Pakhtunkhwa Textbook Board, 2013), p. 88.

18. Choudhary and Azam, *Pakistan Studies: Class 9*, p. 128.

19. Rizvi and others, *Pakistan Studies for Secondary Classes: Class IX–X*, p. 244.

20. Aftab Ahmad Dar, *Pakistan Studies: Class 10* (Lahore, Pakistan: Gohar Publishers, 2013), p. 30.

21. Ibid., p. 42.

22. Ibid., p. 49.

23. Ibid., p. 106.

24. Ahsan Butt, "Nationalistic Narratives in Pakistani Textbooks," Peace Brief 210 (Washington: United States Institute of Peace, 2016).

25. A. H. Nayyar and Ahmed Salim, *The Subtle Subversion: The State of Curricula and Textbooks in Pakistan* (Islamabad: Sustainable Development Policy Institute, 2003).

26. Pervez Hoodbhoy, "Is It Science or Theology?," *Dawn*, May 7, 2016 (www.dawn.com/news/1256797).

27. Ullah, *Vying for Allah's Vote: Understanding Islamic Parties, Political Violence, and Extremism in Pakistan*, p. 86, quoting Shiraz Thobani, *Islam in the School Curriculum: Symbolic Pedagogy and Cultural Claims* (London: Continuum, 2010), pp. 33–34.

28. Dar, *Pakistan Studies: Class 10* (Gohar Publishers, 2013), p. 25.

29. Lant Pritchett, Michael Woolcock, and Matt Andrews, "Capability Traps? The Mechanisms of Persistent Implementation Failure," Working Paper 234 (Washington: Center for Global Development, December 2010).

30. "Siraj Demands Education Emergency," November 30, 2015 (https://jamaat.org/en/news_detail.php?article_id=436).

31. Bureau of Statistics, *Punjab Development Statistics* (Lahore, Pakistan: Government of the Punjab, 2013) (www.bos.gop.pk/?q=system /files/Dev-2013.pdf).

32. See Jane Perlez, "Pakistani Army, Shaken by Raid, Faces New Scrutiny," *New York Times*, May 4, 2011.

33. See Jane Perlez, "Pakistan's Army Chief Warns U.S. on Another Raid," *New York Times*, May 6, 2011.

34. For a discussion of some common conspiracy theories, see Robert Mackey, "A Grand Conspiracy Theory from Pakistan," *New York Times*, Lede blog, May 12, 2009 (http://thelede.blogs.nytimes.com/2009/05/12/a-grand-conspiracy-theory-from-pakistan).

35. Alan B. Krueger, *What Makes a Terrorist: Economics and the Roots of Terrorism* (Princeton University Press, 2008).

36. Sir Michael Barber, "The Good News from Pakistan" (London: Reform, July 2013), p. 33.

37. Chris Kenrick, "Poverty, Illiteracy Cause Terrorism—Musharraf," *Palo Alto Online*, January 17, 2009 (https://www.paloaltoonline.com/news/2009/01/17/poverty-illiteracy-cause-terrorism-8211-musharraf).

38. John May, "Pakistan's Demographic Challenges," *Center For Global Development*, January 7, 2013 (https://www.cgdev.org/blog/pakistan%E2%80%99s-demographic-challenges).

39. Cambridge International Examinations, "Cambridge O Level Pakistan Studies 2059: Syllabus for Examination in 2015," Cambridge, U.K.: 2013 (www.cie.org.uk/programmes-and-qualifications/cambridge-o-level-pakistan-studies-2059/).

40. Nigel Kelly, *The History and Culture of Pakistan* (London: Peak Publishing, 2015), p. 77.

41. Ibid., p. 114.

42. Ibid., p. 118.

43. Ibid., p. 132.

44. Ibid., p. 187.

45. Ibid., p. 7.

46. Ibid., p. 9.

47. Imtiaz Ali, "How a Student of Elite Institutions Turned to Terrorism, JIT Reveals," *Dawn*, May 13, 2016 (www.dawn.com/news/1257959).

Chapter 5

1. Haroon K. Ullah, *Vying for Allah's Vote: Understanding Islamic Parties, Political Violence, and Extremism in Pakistan*, South Asia in World Affairs Series (Georgetown University Press, 2014), p. 87.

2. Husain Haqqani, "Islamism and the Pakistani State," *Current Trends in Islamist Ideology* 15 (August 9, 2013), pp. 25–34.

3. Hassan Abbas, *The Taliban Revival: Violence and Extremism on the Pakistan-Afghanistan Frontier* (Yale University Press, 2015); Ullah, *Vying for Allah's Vote.*

4. Ullah, *Vying for Allah's Vote,* p. 142.

5. Ibid., p. 91.

6. "Profile: Maulana Fazlur Rahman," BBC.com, November 6, 2002, sec. South Asia (http://news.bbc.co.uk/2/hi/south_asia/2411683.stm).

7. Zia Ur Rehman, "Fallout," *The Friday Times,* October 31, 2014 (www.thefridaytimes.com/tft/fallout/).

8. "Fazl Escapes Second Attack in Two Days," *Dawn,* March 31, 2011 (www.dawn.com/2011/03/31/fazl-escapes-second-attack-in-two-days).

9. The PNA consisted of three Islamist parties (Jamaat-e-Islami, the Jamiat Ulema-e-Pakistan, and the Jamaat-ahle-Sunnat), four leftist parties (the Communist Party of Pakistan, the Baluch National Party, the Milli Awami Party, and the Awami National Party), a center-right party (Pakistan Muslim League), and a new party on the right (Tehrik-e-Istaqlal).

10. Seyyed Vali Reza Nasr, *The Vanguard of the Islamic Revolution: The Jama'at-i Islami of Pakistan,* Comparative Studies on Muslim Societies 19 (University of California Press, 1994).

11. The MMA included the Jamaat-e-Islami, the Jamiat Ulema-e-Islam Sami, the Jamiat Ulema-e-Islam Fazl, the Jamiat Ulema-e-Pakistan, the Jamiat-ahle-Hadith, and the Islami Tehrik Pakistan.

12. Madiha Afzal, "Do Barriers to Candidacy Reduce Political Competition? Evidence from a Bachelor's Degree Requirement for Legislators in Pakistan," *Public Choice* 161, no. 1–2 (October 2014), pp. 51–72, doi:10.1007/s11127-013-0126-2.

13. William Dalrymple, "Days of Rage: Challenges for the Nation's Future," *New Yorker,* July 23, 2007 (www.newyorker.com/magazine/2007/07/23/days-of-rage).

14. Ismail Khan, "PESHAWAR: MMA Govt Fails to Meet Provisions: Shariat Bill," *Dawn,* July 25, 2003 (http://beta.dawn.com/news/131826/peshawar-mma-govt-fails-to-meet-provisions-shariat-bill).

15. Joshua T. White, *Pakistan's Islamist Frontier: Islamic Politics and U.S. Policy in Pakistan's North-West Frontier,* Religion and Security Monograph Series, no. 1 (Arlington, Va.: Center on Faith and International Affairs, 2008), p. 52.

16. Ibid., p. 53.

17. Ibid., p. 57.

18. Ibid., p. 54.

19. Owais Tohid, "Interview: Maulana Fazlur Rehman," *Newsline*, accessed July 19, 2016 (http://newslinemagazine.com/magazine/interview-maulana-fazlur-rehman/).

20. Abbas, *The Taliban Revival*, p. 147.

21. White, *Pakistan's Islamist Frontier: Islamic Politics and U.S. Policy in Pakistan's North-West Frontier*; Matthew J. Nelson, "Islamist Politics in South Asia after the Arab Spring: Parties and Their Proxies Working with—and against—the State," Rethinking Political Islam (Brookings Institution, August 2015).

22. National Commission on Terrorist Attacks upon the United States, Thomas H. Kean, and Lee Hamilton, *The 9/11 Commission Report* (Washington: National Commission on Terrorist Attacks upon the United States, 2004).

23. Ullah, *Vying for Allah's Vote*, p. 93.

24. Ibid., p. 144.

25. Tahir Andrabi and others, "Religious School Enrollment in Pakistan: A Look at the Data," *Comparative Education Review* 50(3) (2006), pp. 446–77, doi:10.1086/503885.

26. Tahir Andrabi, Jishnu Das, and Asim Ijaz Khwaja, "The Madrassa Controversy: The Story Does Not Fit the Facts," in *Under the Drones: Modern Lives in Afghanistan-Pakistan Borderlands* (Harvard University Press, 2012), pp. 162–73.

27. Ibid.

28. Andrabi and others, "Religious School Enrollment in Pakistan."

29. Ibid.

30. Ullah, *Vying for Allah's Vote*, p. 34.

31. Ibid., p. 142.

32. Peter W. Singer, "Pakistan's Madrassahs: Ensuring a System of Education Not Jihad," November 1, 2001 (www.brookings.edu/research/papers/2001/11/pakistan-singer).

33. "293 Punjab Seminaries Linked to Terrorism," *The Nation*, November 26, 2015 (http://nation.com.pk/national/26-Nov-2015/293-punjab-seminaries-linked-to-terrorism).

34. Saleem H. Ali, *Islam and Education: Conflict and Conformity in Pakistan's Madrassahs* (Oxford University Press, 2009), p. 37.

35. Ibid., p. 62.

36. Ibid., p. 108.

37. Ibid., p. 83.

38. Tariq Rahman, *Denizens of Alien Worlds: A Study of Education, Inequality, and Polarization in Pakistan* (Oxford University Press, 2004), p. 88.

39. Ibid.

40. Azhar Hussain, Aḥmad Salim, and Arif Naveed, "Connecting the Dots: Education and Religious Discrimination in Pakistan. A Study of Public Schools and Madrassas" (Washington, D.C.: United States Commission on International Religious Freedom, November 2011), p. 52.

41. Ali, *Islam and Education*, p. 86.

42. Tariq Rahman, "Denizens of Alien Worlds: A Survey of Students and Teachers at Pakistan's Urdu and English Language-Medium Schools, and Madrassas," *Contemporary South Asia* 13, no. 3 (2004), pp. 307–29. These numbers and those that follow are derived from table B-4.

43. Ali, *Islam and Education*, p. 71.

44. Ibid., p. 142.

45. Ibid., p. 83.

46. Ibid., p. 84.

47. Ibid., p. 64.

48. Nosheen Abbas, "Pakistan's Madrasa Reform 'Stalls,'" *The Guardian*, October 11, 2011, sec. Education (www.theguardian.com /education/2011/oct/11/pakistan-stalls-madrassa-reforms -english).

49. Dawn.com, "2008: Education Ministry Spent $4m of $100m on Madrassa Reform in Six Years," June 12, 2011 (www.dawn.com/2011 /06/12/2008-education-ministry-spent-4m-of-100m-on-madrassa -reform-in-six-years/).

Chapter 6

1. Fatima Bhutto, "ISIS Hates Our Saint Because He Belongs to Everyone," *New York Times*, February 23, 2017.

2. "Why Was a Prominent Muslim Musician Gunned Down in Pakistan?," NPR (www.npr.org/2016/06/26/483231557/why-was-a -prominent-muslim-musician-gunned-down-in-pakistan).

3. Dawn.com, "Army Chief Bajwa Vows Revenge for Sehwan Attacks: 'No More Restraint,'" February 16, 2017 (www.dawn.com/news /1315139).

4. Ibid.

5. Ibid.

6. "Why India Now?," *Newsweek Pakistan*, February 17, 2017 (http://newsweekpakistan.com/why-india-now).

7. Gallup Pakistan, "Talk Show Analysis: January 2015," January 30, 2015 (http://gallup.com.pk/wp-content/uploads/2015/09/Press-Release -January-20151.pdf).

8. "102 Madrassas Sealed for Stoking Sectarianism," *Express Tribune*, November 12, 2015 (https://tribune.com.pk/story/989768/counterterror -plan-102-madrassas-sealed-for-stoking-sectarianism).

9. Madiha Afzal and Anand Patwardhan, "Redefining Pakistan," Brookings Institution, January 11, 2017 (www.brookings.edu/blog/up -front/2017/01/11/redefining-pakistan).

10. See Article 62 of the Constitution of Pakistan (http://www.pak istani.org/pakistan/constitution/part3.ch2.html).

11. Cass R. Sunstein and Adrian Vermeule, "Conspiracy Theories," Harvard Public Law Working Paper No. 08-03, January 15, 2008 (http:// papers.ssrn.com/abstract=1084585).

12. Tahir Andrabi and Jishnu Das, "In Aid We Trust: Hearts and Minds and the Pakistan Earthquake of 2005" (The World Bank Policy Research Working Paper Series 5440, 2010).

13. Alan B. Krueger, *What Makes a Terrorist: Economics and the Roots of Terrorism* (Princeton University Press, 2008).

Appendix A

1. The word "freely" was in the original Objectives Resolution, but it was missing in the annex to the 1973 Constitution once that constitution was revived by Zia's Order No. 14 of 1985; it was reinserted as in the original via the eighteenth amendment to the constitution in 2010.

Index